RUSSIA BY RIVER

MOSCOW↔ST. PETERSBURG
RIVER CRUISE COMPANION

written and researched by

Howard Shernoff
Tanya Samofalova

st. petersburg

ABOUT THE AUTHORS

Howard Shernoff is an American writer and photographer. He is author of *Paradise Displaced: New Poetry and Prose from the New Motherland* as well as eight other books of poetry. He is also co-author of *Beneath the Ashes: Words and Images Inspired by the Mt. Pinatubo Disaster*. He has lived in Russia since 1993, when he spent the river cruise season working aboard the m.s. *Russ*, which sailed the Moscow-St. Petersburg route more times than he can remember.

Tanya Samofalova is an English speaking Russian interpreter and guide. She has lived and worked in the Ukraine, Mari Republic, and Russia. From 1990 to 1993 she served as senior interpreter aboard the m.s. *Russ*, which, during her employment, sailed the Moscow-St. Petersburg route more times than anybody can remember.

The authors reside in St. Petersburg.

SPECIAL THANKS

To m.s. *Russ* Cruise Director Zinaida Petrashova for giving us the opportunity to live *Russia by River* before writing it and for her everlasting friendship; to former m.s. *Surkov* First Chartman Gennadiy Matveyev for spending cold marathon sessions with us in front of navigational maps; to Dima and Dima at Rikki-Tikki-Tavi for being genuine people in the difficult world of Russian publishing; to Donna Newcombe for keeping us afloat in California; and to JoAnn Shernoff for her amazing love and thankless management of our Colorado operations.

Published in St. Petersburg by Rikki-Tikki-Tavi, Inc.
ISBN 5-87490-026-8

RUSSIA BY RIVER: THE PHOTO ALBUM

We are pleased to announce the recent publication of the **Russia by River Photo Album**, the companion to the guidebook.

The Photo Album is a full color, 28 page journal of the Moscow-St. Petersburg route. It contains over fifty brilliant images by award winning photographers Howard Shernoff and Vladimir Filipov. Having traveled up and down the rivers numerous times, the photographers have been able to capture one-of-a-kind landscapes, portraits, and moments of daily life in Russia.

This publication is a limited edition. To order, please send check or

MORE ON THE GUIDEBOOK

We welcome and encourage your comments, any new information you might discover, and mail orders. For additional copies of the *Russia by River* guidebook, please send check or money order for $14.50 ($13.00 plus $1.50 first class shipping and handling) to our United States address.

Russia by River not available on board you ship? Let us know! And don't forget to complain loudly to your cruise director and tour operator— because it's their fault, not ours!

INTERNET

We invite you to visit Russia by River on the Internet to discover more about the book, to view and read about other publications by the authors, and to explore links to other great sites related to cruising Russia! The address is easy: www.russiabyriver.com!

MAILING ADDRESS

Russia by River
PO Box 406
Ridgway, CO 81432 USA

INTRODUCTION

Russia by River is the first and only comprehensive insider's guide dedicated exclusively to the Moscow-St. Petersburg river cruise. It is an indispensable companion for the journey. Without it you are at the mercy of occasional onboard announcements to inform you about where you are and what you are seeing. And you have no record of your remarkable trip. With it you transcend from the plight of dumbfounded tourist to the status of enlightened traveler. Plus you possess a handy keepsake of your voyage.

The book documents practically every point of interest, landmark, and village lying along the 1400 kilometer-long river route. But that's not all. In it you will find succinct yet complete information on every port of call, including Moscow and St. Petersburg. Additionally provided is detailed information about the numerous distinct waterways traveled. Last but not least, it contains useful vignettes on a variety of topics ranging from Russian architecture to souvenir shopping.

Whether you are on the ship taking in the passing Russian countryside from a deck chair or off the ship taking in the nightlife of St. Petersburg, you become in the know with the book in hand. What is the story behind that interesting church on the riverbank? What kinds of fish live in this lake? Where is the most exclusive restaurant in Yaroslavl? How much should I pay for a laquer box? Answers to all questions like these are here.

Having worked on the riverships for many seasons, we trust that this book will at last satisfy the insatiable curiosity most passengers have about the wonderland that is Russia. By offering a mix of relevant statistics, amusing anecdotes, and helpful tips, we hope to add an extra dimension to the unique adventure you have chosen to undertake.

Shchastlivova puteshestviya! Bon voyage!

CONTENTS

THE RIVER ROUTE

This portion of the book is your kilometer by kilometer guide to the sights seen along the banks of the entire river route. Even though you won't be able to use it at all times, as you will likely be sleeping, dining, dancing, and attending lectures during much of the navigation, you might want to read it through once. You will encounter plenty of amusing stories and commentaries which make this section by itself an entertaining introduction to Russian history, geography, and, well, psychology. We kindly ask you to review the following instructions on its proper use.

HOW TO USE THIS SECTION:

Providing a detailed desription of the river route that is user-friendly to all passengers is problematic. Ships travel in two different directions and utilize different iteneraries and timetables. They also travel at varying speeds and encounter unique navigational conditions. Moreover, posted distance markers are sometimes not seen for long stretches. To achieve the best possible continuity, we have employed a system based on the navigational charts used by all ships. This means several things:

(1) **The guide starts from Moscow.** On navigational maps, Moscow's Southern River Terminal is kilometer zero. More important, signposts along the shores of the route are numbered from this point.

(2) **Passengers originating in St. Petersburg therefore begin reading this section on Page 60.** Passengers from St. Petersburg simply read the entries in reverse order. It's a bit of a hassle, but you'll get used to it.

(3) **Port means left; starboard means right. Port is abbreviated "p." Starboard is abbreviated "sb."** These abbreviated terms are used to direct you to the proper side of the ship from which to view a given sight. Passengers from St. Petersburg look to the opposite side of what is indicated.

Therefore, a typical entry looks like this:

"**[KM 833 p]**"... followed by a description of a given point of interest. In this example, the point of interest is located on the port side of the ship 833 kilometers from Moscow. Passengers from Moscow look to the port side as indicated; those from St. Petersburg look to the starboard side.

Applying the distances written in the book to those you are actually passing on board the ship is the difficult part. Once you start using the guide from the deck, however, you quickly become accustomed to how the ship's speed influences the time between landmarks. There are enough reference points described in the guide to allow you to orient yourself at any time.

Furthermore, from time to time you will see kilometer signs on the banks of the route. These signs are actually posted every five kilometers. However, because of varying conditons (wide stretches of river, dense forests, etc.) you may not be able to spot them with consistency. For those intent on following the guide as closely as possible, a pair of binoculars comes in very handy. Even without binoculars, though, you should be able to maintain your bearings fairly easily. Also, don't be afraid to ask your crew for assistance—who do you think is paying those guys, anyway?

Conversions applicable to this section:

1 meter	= 1.09 yards (3.28 feet)
1 kilometer	= 0.62 miles
1 square kilometer	= 0.39 square miles
1 cubic meter	= 1.30 cubic yards

MOSCOW CANAL
(KM 46 – 165)

[KM 46] Welcome to Moscow's **Northern River Terminal**, built in 1937 in "Stalinist Gothic" style to resemble a massive passenger ship. What a combination, eh? The red ruby star atop the 85 meter-high spire supposedly was taken from the Moscow Kremlin. Note the statue of polar bears on the building's northern end and one of dolphins on the southern end. Get the connection? By the way, Moscow kilometer zero is located 46 kilometers and 4 locks farther down the canal at the Southern River Terminal, near the Kremlin. Hence your voyage technically begins at kilometer 46. Watch for signs every five kilometers along the banks to help keep you oriented.

[KM 46-8 sb] Moscow's **Northern Cargo Port,** one of three in the city, sprawls along the bank. Gigantic loading cranes, which service ships from as far away as the Caspian and Baltic seas, stand in strangely animated postures along the port. If you spot a large concrete and metal warehouse, you've spied the biggest refrigerator in Moscow, where tons of fish are kept before moving on to collect flies in the shops downtown.

[KM 48] The **Leningrad Highway Bridge** marks the joining of the **Moscow Canal** proper to the **Khimky Reservoir**, on which the Northern River Terminal is located.

[KM 49] A region of Moscow called **Khimky** gains access to the other side of the reservoir via the **Moscow Circular Highway Bridge**, which marks the Moscow city limit. Khimky, which formerly was an independent settlement, was the sight of equestrian events during the 1980 Olympics. It is also where user-unfriendly Sheremetyevo Airport is located.

[KM 50] The ship passes under the **October Railway Bridge**, built in 1935. The clearance below the bridge sets the maximum height of canal-going vessels at 13.6 meters.

[KM 51-7] Verdant banks slope down both sides of the canal along this dramatic section called **Glubokaya Viyemka**, or "Deep Hollow." To establish a depth here of 23 meters, canal diggers scooped out enough soil to fill a train reaching to Vladivostock. The depth of the cut is connected to the fact that you're sailing through a mountain.

[KM 60 sb] A monument in the form of a hydrofoil stands at the entrance to a large shipyard. This area is called the **Khlebnikovo Backwater**, formed by the mouth of the **Klyazma River**, and it's where some of the Moscow River Shipping Company fleet spends its winters. The adjacent town of **Khlebnikovo** boasts one of the regions most popular holiday rest homes, located on the embankment.

[KM 65 p] The village of **Troitskoye** features a small church and yacht club, which can be seen along the shore. And yes, the term "yacht club" is being applied loosely. On the starboard side, near shore, floats a severed Aeroflot jet. A free copy of the *Russia by River Photo Album* awaits anyone who can tell us why.

[KM 66] The canal enters the **Klyazminskoye Reservoir**. On the bank is the village of **Novosetsovo**.

[KM 66-71 sb] Along this stretch of crooked canal you'll pass a village called **Khverevo**, situated behind a pier. Four miles inland from this spot lies the village of **Zhostovo**, where those Russian painted trays you see being peddled in souvenir shops are made.

[KM 72 sb] An inlet leads back to the **Uchinskoye Reservoir**, an off-limits area constituting Volga waters in the process of "settling" before being piped from here to the Moscow Water Station for purification. In other words, it's kind of a cesspool. On the opposite shore of the **Pyalovskoye Reservoir**, on which the ship is now sailing, a bay is formed by the mouth of the **Ucha River**. This is a popular recreation spot called **Solnechnaya Polyana**, or "Sunny Clearing." More noteworthy is the village of **Fedoskino**, situated atop the river bank, but unfortunately not very visible from the ship. This is one of the four Russian villages that produce hand-painted lacquer boxes (see p. 202). Legend has it that lacquer box production started in Fedoskino when a merchant named Korobov began lacquering the bills of hats for Russian soldiers. He then went on to make snuff boxes and, eventually, all kinds of little boxes. A school, opened here in 1931, continues to preserve the tradition of lacquer box painting.

[KM 74-7 sb] The settlement of **Vitenevo** lies along the shore of this short stretch of canal between reservoirs. The Russian writer Saltykov-Shchedrin kept a mansion here; it was flooded when the reservoir was filled.

[KM 77-82] This 11.5 square kilometer basin is called the **Pestovskoye Reservoir**, on which you'll see a number of islands. Before this area was flooded, the islands were hilltops. Passenger ships heading for Moscow often tie up at the pier in front of **Pine Grove** (*Sosnoviy bor*). The reason for the stop is that ships often are too early for their strictly allocated arrival time in Moscow and thus have some time to kill. You will likely be allowed to disembark for a few hours to stroll through the lovely forest here. We recommend it, as this is the last hint of nature before reaching the concrete jungle of Moscow. If there happens to be a Russian ship also docked here, her passengers might be found out in the forest picking berries. Americans, who think that berries grow in little cartons beneath plastic wrap, are probably better off not following them to harvest the vegetation. Look out for elks, hares, squirrels, and foxes, which are said to prowl around the more dense areas.

[KM 82-6] Along this short stretch of canal that connects two reservoirs lie the villages of **Protasovo** and

Rozhdestvino. The latter is identifiable by its hydrofoil moorage and a striking stone church and belfry.

[KM 86-92] Handsome two- and three-story cottages dot the banks of the **Ikshinskoye Reservoir**, on which the ship sails. The dwellings belong to the village of **Bolshoye Ivanovskoye**, which has charge of the nice farmland. Incidentally, some document somewhere says something about people living in this area 4,000 years ago. Isn't that something?

[KM 93] Some sources refer to the sculpted figures atop the lower towers of **Lock # 6** as Soviet workers, while others identify them as canal builders. They're probably not very representative of either, as Soviet laborers tended to exhibit a more downcast look, and canal builders typically were GULAG political prisoners. The lock measures 290m x 30m x 15.5m. The net change in water level here is 8 meters. St. Petersburg-bound ships drop; Moscow-bound ships rise. Depending on your direction, this is either the first or last lesson of your Russian locking education.

[KM 93-6 p] The settlement of **Iksha** lies behind the highway and railroad that run parallel to the canal between the fifth and sixth locks.

[KM 96] In front of the upper towers of **Lock # 5** stands a statue of a young woman holding aloft a model of a sailboat. Exactly who she is and what she's doing here is unclear, so she therefore fits in nicely with the rest of the intriguing lock adornments found along the canal. This lock features some flashy architectural styles also. Notice the enclosed galleries in the upper towers. Planted atop the lower towers are small colonnaded belvederes. Around the lower part of the lock a granite staircase is decorated with urns and iron grillwork. According to official information, all these elements were incorporated to foster the lock's "harmony with the surrounding greenness of the Iksha River Valley." The lock measures 290m x 30m x 15.5m. The net change in water level here is 8 meters. St. Petersburg-bound ships drop; Moscow-bound ships rise.

[KM 103] Situated in a picturesque valley, **Lock # 4** sports glass-enclosed observation decks in its towers (although they're not as spiffy as they sound). The lock's dimensions are 290m x 30m x 15.5m. The net change in water level here is 8 meters. St. Petersburg-bound ships drop; Moscow-bound ships rise.

[KM 104 sb] On the southern side of the **Savelovskiy Railway Bridge**, the **Yakhroma Reservoir** recedes back to the village of **Ilyinskoye**.

[KM 106 p] The **Yakhroma River** is grafted onto the canal.

[KM 107] Keeping up the tradition of curious items adorning the canal's locks, the lower towers of **Lock # 3** are crowned with beautiful replicas of Christopher Columbus's famous galleon the *Santa Maria*. To round out the apparent incongruity, the upper towers used to bear shiny hammer-and-sickle emblems. The lock measures 290m x 30m x 15.5m. The net change in water level here is 8 meters. St. Petersburg-bound ships drop; Moscow-bound ships rise.

[KM 108 p] The city of **Yakhroma** grew out of a 19th century settlement which operated one of the region's first textile plants. The factory is still functioning today, having been somewhat renovated, one would hope. The **Yakhroma Bridge**, which connects the factory to the city, was the site of WWII heroics, as evidenced by a bronze soldier standing on a granite base at the eastern approach to the bridge.

[KM 108-15 p] The **Yakhroma River** flows parallel to the canal.

[KM 115 sb] The church seen standing behind all the cranes in the port of **Dmitrov** is the Assumption Cathedral, built in the 16th century. Its architecture is reminiscent of that of the Archangel Michael Cathedral in the Moscow Kremlin. But that's not all Dmitrov has in common with the capital. The two cities were founded by the same prince, Yury Dolgoruky (the Long-armed), who first came here on a tax-collecting mission in 1154. Dolgoruky was traveling with a princess, who according to history, "along the way gave birth to a son, Dmitry." So the prince founded a fortress called Dmitrov, which eventually grew into a city. The city itself was one of Russia's largest and most populated in the 15th and 16th centuries, but later underwent a long period of decline. In the 1920s, it was a quiet little town of 5,000 people. In the 1930s, it became Moscow Canal construction headquarters and exploded into a demi-metropolis of 60,000 people.

[KM 127-30 sb] The village of **Nadezhdino** (derived from *nadezhda*, meaning "hope") lies at the north end of this long, narrow bend in the canal. Navigators are busy communicating with each other here to avoid collisions.

[KM 151] The banks beside **Lock # 2** are known to feature some pretty impressive landscaping. You might see some flower beds, fountains, and decorative lattice. The operable phrase here is "you might." As for the figures on the lock towers, on the left we have three rank-and-file Soviet workers; on the right the threesome is comprised of a pilot, a soldier, and a border guard. What they're all doing up there is anybody's guess. The lock itself measures 290m x 30m x 13.5m. The net change in water level here is 6 meters. St. Petersburg-bound ships drop; Moscow-bound ships rise.

[KM 160] The **Sestra River**, or "Sister River," crosses the canal. Note that the river has been diverted beneath the canal.

[KM 162 sb] As the ship turns near the lock, you'll see the **Big Volga Lighthouse**.

[KM 164 p] On the shore amidst the trees stands **Lenin**.

Many ships pass him in the dead of night, so in case you miss him, here is one recent passenger's impression: "A very granite father of socialism is striking an observant, grandfatherly pose, his gaze on Mother Volga. One hand rests behind his back, as if concealing something, the other is outstretched, as if it should be holding a snifter of cognac. Flowers rise up from the base of the statue, while from the head streams down bird excrement. If you look back after passing the figure, it appears as if Lenin has three legs."

[KM 165] The **Volga River** is joined to the **Moscow Canal** by **Lock # 1** of the Moscow Canal. Lock buffs might take note of the unique cylindrical flood gates at the bottom of the lock chamber. The dimensions of the chamber are 290m x 30m x 18.5m. The net change in water level here is 11 meters. St. Petersburg-bound ships drop; Moscow-bound ships rise.

(KM 46 – 165)

⬆ MOSCOW CANAL ⬆

VOLGA RIVER
(KM 166 – 385)

[KM 166-73 sb] The city of **Dubna** actually is situated on an island surrounded by the Dubna and Sestra rivers, the Volga River, and the Moscow Canal. It is what the Soviets called a "science town," which means that it was built in the mid-20th century around a scientific research facility. The facility here is the Institute for Nuclear Research. Before reaching the institute, you will pass a long stretch of typical Soviet highrises facing grand, "new Russian" *dachas* under construction across the river. Then come an indoor swimming pool, a patch of pleasant beach, and a colorful boat storage area. Well before reaching Dubna you might notice a big sign on the shore reading "Dubna" in Russian. This marker demarcates the region of Dubna rather than the city proper.

[KM 175 sb] On the outskirts of Dubna, where the mouth of the **Dubna River** joins the Volga, are a church and a horse ranch.

[KM 185-92]   Ships originating in St. Petersburg are required to stop for a sanitary inspection at the city of **Kimry**. According to regulations designed to safeguard the water of the Moscow Canal, inspectors board the ships to seal the "dark water" tanks. Usually ships purify their own "dark water" and expel it along the way. The water of the Moscow Canal, being devoid of much current, is rather fragile, so as a precaution ships have to "hold it in" until they reach a purification plant at the capital.

Sanitation issues aside, Kimry itself, rather desolate from the river, boasts a fairly fascinating history. First documented in the mid-16th century when it was a trading center for fish, poultry, and bread, Kimry in the 17th century became a center of shoe production. Why? Because a cattle-herding route went right by the city. Shoes and boots became Kimry's bread and butter for the next three hundred years. Local literature claims that Kimry shoes are as famous as Tula samovars, Vologda lace, and Ivanovo linen. And who could dispute that? After all, Kimry boots were worn by Peter the Great's soldiers, and it was "in Kimry boots that the Soviet Army reached Berlin" (from a local guidebook). In the 19th century, when over 15,000 shoe-makers inhabited the city, it hosted a semi-annual footwear trade fair. Kimry shoemakers constituted an elite peasant class who took pride in their dress and decorum. They also enjoyed imbibing large quantities of vodka, perhaps giving birth to the Russian expression "drunk as a cobbler." During Soviet times, all of the shoe manufacturers were "united" under the label Red Star, which still turns out shoes and boots designed primarily for mountaineers and geologists. The Red Star popular line, however, has been suffering for years from shortages and poor quality of natural resources. But who knows, with the rush to capitalistic embrace, maybe Kimry will spawn Russia's answer to Nike. Any guesses as to what is featured prominently on Kimry's coat of arms?

[KM 200 sb] An aged church, flanked by monstrous power lines, stands near the village of **Beloye**.

[KM 205 sb] Directly across from the kilometer marker rests an old stern-wheeler, formerly used as a holiday rest home. To the right stands the white stone St. George Church, surrounded by scaffolding. It's probable that at one time most of the buildings around here were made of white stone, as this is the town of **Beliy Gorodok**, or "White Town," settled in the 14th century. Today the town is engaged in ship repairing and is a winter port to the Moscow Shipping Company fleet.

[KM 219 p] The village of **Medveditskoye** lies at the mouth of the **Medveditsa River**, where there once stood a mighty fortress, now in ruins. This was a popular place for fortifications, as the river for centuries served as border between the Tver and Novgorod principalities.

[KM 231 sb] The village of **Sknyatino**, situated at the mouth of the **Nerl River**, was founded by Yury Dolgoruky, the same prince who founded Moscow. Ever since its first mention in the Chronicles in 1134, Sknyatino was considered a lovely city, so much so that the princes of the Kiev and Vladimir-Suzdal principalities constantly fought over it. By fighting for it, naturally, they destroyed it. During the next century, it was rebuilt, but then Mongol-Tatars burned it to the ground. It seems never to have recovered.

[KM 238 sb] Some ships make their "green stop" here on the shores of **Novookatovo**. A smattering of *dachas*, a park, a pier, and a sanatorium lie along the banks.

[KM 244 sb] You might be able to catch a glimpse of a bust of Pushkin in front of a mansion in the village of **Nikitskoye**. As there seem to be monuments to the revered writer wherever he set foot, he probably spent some time at the mansion.

[KM 249 p] The mouth of the **Kashinka River** enters on the north side of the **Kashinskiy Bridge**. On this bridge the St. Petersburg-Moscow railroad crosses the Volga.

[KM 260 sb] Probably the most popular shipboard photo-opportunity, the **flooded belfry of Kalyazin** stands singularly amidst the waters, constituting what one local observer calls "a beautiful and sad sight." The beauty of the stranded structure is easily seen; the sadness requires explanation. The belfry, which formerly stood 70 meters high and was considered among the tallest and finest structures along the Volga, was erected in 1800 as part of the St. Nicholas Cathedral on Kalyazin's Market Square. You are now sailing *over* Market Square, which was flooded in order to dam the river at the Uglich Hydroplant. The upper portion of the belfry, recently planted on an unattractive earthen foundation, is all that survives.

Behind the belfry, around the mouth of the **Zhabnya River**, lies the town of **Kalyazin**, which suffered much the same fate as its belfry. The town sprung up around the Kalyazin Monastery, founded in the 15th century by Saint Makary on land donated by a converted feudal lord, Ivan Kolyaga. By the 16th century the monastery had become among the richest in Russia. Tsar Ivan IV (the Terrible) personally visited and donated rare manuscripts to the monastery's library. In the 20th century Tsar Josef Stalin also visited—in the form of Soviet dynamite that blew up the place. Much of Kalyazin was forced to move to the higher bank, as the low-lying portions were flooded. Some original frescoes from the monastery's cathedral are preserved in the city's Museum of Local Studies.

[KM 280 p] At the mouth of the **Puksha River** sits the village of **Priulky**, featuring a lovely, five-domed church.

[KM 280-98] Throughout this 18 kilometer stretch of Volga (and even beyond) the west bank rises high above the water in sharp precipices, while on the eastern shore thick forests extend to the edge of the low bank. The **Vyrezka** and **Pavlovka** rivers join the Volga along the way.

[KM 298-302 p] Along this crooked stretch of river lie the villages of **Kotovo** and **Korozhechno** as well as a couple of churches, one of which is in derelict condition.

[KM 310] Entering the lock of the **Uglich Hydroplant**, ships pass through a triumphal arch, built to commemorate victory over Germany. The facility, completed in 1940, is operated by only two personnel. The lock itself measures 290m x 30m x 18.5m. The net change in water level here is 11 meters. St. Petersburg-bound ships drop; Moscow-bound ships rise.

[KM 312] The ship ties up at the high embankment of the ancient city of **Uglich**. To the right, in the old kremlin, the splendid Church of St. Dmitry on the Blood with its star-studded cupolas and the green-domed Transfiguration Cathedral await your inspection.

[KM 313 sb] Adjacent to Uglich, in the village of **Zolotoruchye**, a dashing, multi-domed church complements those of the Uglich embankment.

[KM 315 p] Only a few kilometers from Uglich, the Volga bends ninety degrees at the mouth of the **Korozhechna River**.

[KM 320 p] The village of **Voskresenskaya**, or "Resurrection," features a church of the same name.

[KM 344 sb] Across from the mouth of the **Yukhot River** stands a pier to which usually is tied a boat used for ferrying. Behind the pier, perched atop of the bank, the ancient town of **Myshkino** looks out over the Volga. The town boasts a colorful if not somewhat sad past, beginning with the legend of its founding. One day a local feudal lord, out hunting in the woods, grew weary and fell asleep. He was awakened by a mouse scampering over his face. Looking around, the lord saw a snake poised to attack. He killed the snake and ordered a chapel built on the spot where the mouse had saved his life. The settlement was called Myshkino, derived from the Russian word *myshka*, or "little mouse." Myshkino grew to be a bustling town with a unique character. Enterprising merchants, skillful smiths, and inventive potters were among the population which strolled along multi-colored stone streets lined with some of the Volga's finest mansions and cathedrals. Then came the 1917 Bolshevik Revolution and the ensuing communist government. In an attempt to escape the devastating socialist taxes, Myshkino appealed to Moscow to be reclassified as a village rather than a city. Moscow consented, making sure however that the former city would look like a village. Its farmland was collectivized, the local theater, gallery, and museum were closed, and a blanket of Soviet grayness settled over the town. In the 1970s, construction of a gas pipeline began in the region, and a series of concrete buildings was erected on the city's outskirts amidst mosquito-infested marshland to house the influx of new workers. Sadly, the story of Myshkino, according to one historian, "reflects the fate of so many provincial cities that lost their regional face [during the Soviet era]."

[KM 347 sb] A modest church stands in the small village of **Okhotino**.

[KM 363 sb] The ship passes a typical Volga village, **Gorodok**, with a typical Volga church.

[KM 367 p] A four-section railway bridge spans the river at the village of **Volga**. A few pillars might be sticking out of the water around here; they're remnants of an older bridge.

[KM 372 sb] A neglected brick church stands in the village of **Ivanovskoye**.

[KM 385 sb] The village of **Koprino** marks the division between the **Rybinsk Reservoir** and the **Volga River**.

(KM 166-385)
⬆ VOLGA RIVER ⬆

DOWN THE VOLGA
TO YAROSLAVL AND KOSTROMA
–not traveled by all ships–

NOTE ON KILOMETER INDICATING SYSTEM: Because this segment of the journey is a side trip of sorts, kilometers are counted separately from those of the rest of the trip. To maintain consistency with the actual navigational charts used by riverships, this section commences tallying Volga kilometers from an invisible reference point called the Bermuda Triangle in the south of the Rybinsk Reservoir. The Bermuda Triangle is located 410 kilometers from Moscow. Thus the trip down the Volga begins at **KM 410**, here referred to as **VOLGA 410**. The net addition of the Volga round trip to your overall total is about 380 kilometers.

[**VOLGA 410**] Actually located in the Rybinsk Reservoir, this is the southeastern tip of the **Bermuda Triangle**, an invisible chartsmen reference point from which the voyage down the Volga technically starts.

[**VOLGA 422 sb**] At the approach to the Rybinsk Hydroplant, **Mother Volga** extends a welcoming hand. In her other hand she holds a scroll of some kind, likely the draft plan for the harnessing of the Volga's waters for electricity. A famous Lenin quotation about the electrization of the country used to be inscribed on the base of the monument. Thus, this isn't exactly a gracious monument to the natural mighty Volga, but rather more of a tribute to socialist imposition on nature. It is somehow an inspiring figure nonetheless. Ships passing Mother Volga late at night sometimes illuminate her with their spotlights, allowing passengers to wonder about that giant petrel flying around Mother Volga's shins.

[VOLGA 423] The ship glides beneath a pedestrian over-pass at the approach to the impressive **Rybinsk Hydroplant**. Technically, the hydroplant is located in two rivers, neither of which are here anymore. The dam and hydrostation lie in the old mouth of the Sheksna River, and the lock in the former bed of the Volga. The entire hydroplant wasn't officially completed until 1950, although during WWII it was one of the only sources of Moscow's electricity. (Its snow-filled, unfinished appearance spared it from Luftwaffe attacks.) The hydroplant consists of two separate and parallel locks, **Lock # 11** and **Lock # 12**. Each measures 290m x 30m x 21m. Ships heading down the Volga drop 14 meters.

[VOLGA 424] Exiting the lock, ships navigate the waters of the **Volga River**. Once past the upcoming city of Rybinsk, the stretch of river all the way to Kostroma is known to navigators as the "tea part" of the journey. Why? Because it's such a nice, wide, deep stretch of river that they can sit back, relax, and have tea, of course.

[VOLGA 425-40] With a population of around 300,000, the city of **Rybinsk** and its suburbs stretch along both banks of the Volga. No stranger to Russian naming games, the city's name was changed to Shcherbakov (a Party notable) in 1946, then changed to Andropov after the former general secretary's death in 1984. During *perestroika*, it once again became *Rybinsk* ("Fish Town"), the name most closely associated with the settlement's origins as a 12th century Slavic fishing center. Rybinsk officially became a city in 1777, after Peter the Great's Mariinskaya Canal System had made the settlement an important trading port. Wheat was the major trade here; even today ships laden with wheat can be seen in the port. The scene of yesteryear, however, was likely much livelier, as noted by a 1915 observer: "With the opening of the navigation, the bread starts to arrive, and the

Volga here, a full half kilometer in width, is covered by all sorts of ships, which from afar seem to be a bridge on which one could walk from one bank to the other."

An unmistakable sight in Rybinsk is the Neo-Classical, five-domed Savior-Transfiguration Cathedral with its towering Baroque belfry and dramatic, gilded spire. Built in the mid-19th century, the cathedral could have ended up in St. Petersburg's St. Isaac's Square but that its plan was rejected in favor of that of the present St. Isaac's Cathedral. Other prominent structures along Rybinsk's right bank include the colonnaded, blue and white River Terminal, built in 1811; the New Bread Exchange, an immaculately restored, 20th century, German-style tiled palace perched at the river front; and a 28 meter-high obelisk to local WWII heroes. On the outskirts of the city lies an expansive shipyard with tankers and hydrofoils. Beyond the shipyard stretches a network of oil docks and refineries. Finally, past the Rybinsk city limit a more natural setting is encountered, as old pioneer camps, sanatoriums, and health spas dot the shores.

[VOLGA 448 p] Through a gap in the trees you should be able to glimpse a dilapidated white 18th century mansion called **Tikhvinskoye**, built in 1767. Allegedly one of the region's first examples of "Russian Classical" architecture, the structure's history is as amusing as the name of its style. It seems that a military officer and aspiring aristocrat named Tushinin built the mansion in order to repose in its library with a glass of brandy and a good novel and feel like a man of taste and distinction—and to invite guests over to witness him being a man of taste and distinction. Upon hearing that Catherine the Great was going to be traveling the Volga, Tushinin became obsessed with the dream of hosting the empress at his estate. He wanted to impress her too with his manner of taste and distinction. He was prepared to spare no expense and was aiming to alert the local media of his social coup, but alas, his plans never materialized. Too bad for Catherine, sounds like it would have been right up her alley. Tushinin also erected a one-domed church and a spired, brick belfry, both of which are clearly visible.

[VOLGA 449 sb] On a verdant hilltop near a pier marking the village of **Krasnoye** stand the remains of what was once an elegantly tall and narrow church. It was built in 1724 by a merchant loyal to Peter the Great in the Petrine Baroque style, of course.

[VOLGA 453 sb] The town of **Pesochnoye** (derived from the Russian *pesok*, or "sand") is known for its porcelain manufactory, a sprawling complex of rundown red brick buildings and smokestacks built in 1884. From appearances, it seems doubtful that the factory is still operable and that the art of porcelain painting still thrives here. But in Russia one never knows.

[VOLGA 455 p] The village of **Shashkovo** is where ancestors of that man of taste and distinction, Tushinin, lived. An elegant, Neo-Classical brick church, built in 1775, and an early 19th century belfry stand on the bank.

[VOLGA 460 p] Amidst the trees hide five brown domes belonging to the Epiphany Church in the village of **Khopylevo**.

[VOLGA 467 p] The churches keep coming. The red brick Church of Archangel Michael (1779) with tiny dark cupolas and a spired belfry stands in the village of **Savinskoye** adjacent to a grassy clearing.

[VOLGA 472 sb] And coming. In the village of **Bogoslovskoye** stands the striking Church of St. John the Divine (1882), featuring copper cupolas and accompanied by a towering, red brick belfry, visible from kilometers away.

[VOLGA 480-3 p] The church-strewn town of **Tutaev** is

named after Red Army hero Ilya Tutaev. It was originally called Romanov, as it was founded in 1283 by Yaroslavl Prince Roman. It's entirely possible that by the time you pass it, it will be called Romanov once again. The town flourished in the late 18th century when it's populace comprised icon painters, silversmiths, carpenters, weavers, and boatmakers. During this period, its numerous churches were erected. The particularly striking, cherry-colored Church of the Exaltation of the Cross stands close to the water as if plucked from a Russian fairy tale. Perched on the high bank is the Kazan Transfiguration Church with its white belfry. You might also catch a glimpse of the modest, one-domed Intercession Church and the Savior's Archangel Church. On the opposite bank stands the 17th century Ascension Cathedral. Known for "preserving the feel of the Russian provinces," Tutaev used to be popular with artists, who came here to paint the avenues of old mansions and ornately carved wooden houses.

[**VOLGA 488 sb**] Set back from the bank in the town of **Konstantinovskoye** is the Mendeleyev Chemical Plant, named after the famous Russian scientist who developed the Periodic Table of Elements. According to Soviet literature, a revolutionary lubricant of some kind was developed at the plant in 1879. According to Soviet sources, when the lubricant outclassed American ones on the world market, Americans began printing the words "Just Like Russian Lubricants" on theirs.

[**VOLGA 495 sb**] Before the Volga makes a gradual ninety degree bend, you can catch sight of the domes and spires of a dilapidated, medieval-looking church outside the village of **Petropolovskoye**.

[**VOLGA 502 p**] The **Eet River** empties into the Volga, and guess what marks the spot? Another nice church.

[**VOLGA 506 sb**] The 13th century town of **Norskoye**,

with two churches, lies on the bank.

[VOLGA 512 p] An extremely picturesque sight, the nearly 700 year-old **Tolga Monastery** stands amidst deciduous forest at the water's edge. The monastery walls, whose towers are crowned by gray spires, enclose two main churches. The striking Savior's Cathedral is topped by a dozen domes surrounding a singularly elevated cupola. The white stone Cathedral of the Introduction to the Temple, supporting five large green cupolas, is neighbored by a one-domed chapel and an elegant belfry capped by a tiny cupola. Hanging in the belfry is the largest bell ever cast by craftsman Fyodor Motorin, whose son went on to cast the gigantic Tsar Bell in the Moscow Kremlin.

According to legend, the monastery was founded in 1314 when its first church was built as a tribute to a miracle that happened on the spot. The tale runs that Bishop Trifon of Yaroslavl, returning from a trip to the White Lake, made camp at the mouth of the Tolga River. During the night he was awakened by a pillar of fire burning on the opposite shore. A footbridge then extended to him from the fire. The bishop walked across the bridge to find that the source of the flames was an icon of the Virgin, suspended in the air. Like a good bishop, he dropped to his knees and prayed heartily for a while. Then he walked back across the bridge to his camp and discovered that all of his belongings were missing. He roused his traveling companions, who upon hearing the bishop's tale, boated across the river to discover the icon along with the bishop's things. When word of the event spread, believers came and built a church to house the icon.

A more believable version of the monastery's inception is that Christian mercenaries wanted to build a church on the spot, but the site already constituted a sacred grove used by native pagans to perform their nature-oriented rituals. The pagans didn't want to convert to Christianity, so the mercenaries cut down the grove and built a church anyway.

The entire monastery complex was closed down by the Bolsheviks in 1926 and subsequently turned into a "labor education colony". In 1988, the monastery was given back to the Orthodox Church, which restored it and turned it into the Tolga Nunnery. The nunnery, which is open to visitors, grows vegetables, raises livestock, and plans to open a convalescence home.

[VOLGA 516-22] The sheer, manicured embankment crowned by colonnaded gazebos belongs to one of the oldest cities on the Volga, **Yaroslavl**, where ships drop anchor for the day. At the top of the bank, a tree-lined promenade overlooks the river. If you simply ignore the river terminal, the appearance of which one local guidebook tries to justify by suggesting that "although modern, is in harmony with the historical constructions of the embankment," you can enjoy a fine Volga panorama from the promenade.

[VOLGA 525 sb] While cruising through the industrial outskirts of Yaroslavl, you'll notice a factory bearing a huge slogan. It reads: "Don't pollute the Volga!" Yet the Volga is visibly at its filthiest around here, an irony apparently lost on all the fisherman floating around here in small bands of rafts.

[VOLGA 533-60] Along this picturesque stretch of river several small villages and churches are set amidst birch, alder, and cherry trees.

[VOLGA 564-9 p] A dam protects the bank from flooding below the village of **Rybnitsy**. In 1841 one Alexander Opekushin was born into serfdom here. He eventually saved enough rubles to buy his freedom and developed his talents as a sculptor. His work became noticed by the right people, and soon he was commissioned to create several prominent statues. Pieces of his that you can see during your trip include the statue of Peter the Great in Petrozavodsk, the

Pushkin statue in Moscow's Pushkin Square, and the supporting figures in the monument to Catherine the Great along St. Petersburg's Nevsky Prospect. Not bad for a disadvantaged country boy.

[VOLGA 571 p] In the town of **Krasniy Profintern** stands an 150 year-old plant which processes starch and syrup.

[VOLGA 597-604] The golden domes sparkling above fortress walls at the mouth of the **Kostroma River** belong to the Ipatievsky Monastery, one of the country's most famous, situated in the town of **Kostroma**. Once docked at the river terminal, you may not see the "white city on seven hills wearing a necklace of green gardens" described by local literature. Although a bit tarnished, Kostroma is regarded as the quintessence of provincial Russia.

[VOLGA 660] In 1995 one or two ships began calling on historic **Plyos**. It is a charming town of only 3,500 inhabitants, picturesque at every step. If it catches on as a major stop along the river route, you can be sure to read more about it in subsequent editions of *Russia by River*.

[VOLGA 920] As very few ships make it all the way down to **Nizhny Novgorod** during the Moscow-St. Petersburg cruise, a detailed navigation south of Kostroma is not included. (For information on Nizhny Novgorod, see the chapter beginning on p. 105.)

NOTE: This segment is to be used from the beginning only (p. 24), as it covers a Volga round trip which commences at the same point for all ships. Using it backwards makes sense only on the return portion of the round trip.

–not traveled by all ships–
DOWN THE VOLGA
⬆ TO YAROSLAVL AND KOSTROMA ⬆

RYBINSK RESERVOIR
(KM 385-528)

[KM 385-528] The ship traverses the **Rybinsk Reservoir** along a north-south axis. Although because of its size it is commonly called the Rybinsk Sea, in actuality this is a massive flood basin covering the natural beds of many different rivers, including the Volga and Sheksna. The flooding of the basin in 1941 by Stalin's engineers was kept under wraps because of the mass destruction, human displacement, and ecological damage it necessitated (see p.164 for more details). Because the reservoir is so large, there is not much to point out sightwise, except for what you are sailing *over*. For example, at the southern end, where a large church and belfry stand on the western shore, you cruise over the point where the Volga used to meet the Mologa River at the ancient city of Mologa. Founded back in the 12th century, Mologa was a colorful regional center known since the 16th century for its lively annual trade fair, reminiscent of Nizhny Novgorod's. At the time of its flooding, it was a declining town of stone and wooden dwellings, many churches, a monastery, and a population of 7,000 people.

Mologa also marks a significant navigational point called the **Bermuda Triangle** by chartmen. It's named such not because ships disappear here, but rather because a few kilometers are "lost" at the intersection of three navigational paths. It's rather complicated, so don't worry about it.

(KM 385-528)
⬆ RYBINSK RESERVOIR ⬆

1.

2.

3.

4.

5.

ALONG THE VOLGA-BALTIC CANAL:
SHEKSNA RIVER AND RESERVOIR
(KM 528 – 714)

[KM 528] Just outside Cherepovets the **Sheksna River** empties into the **Rybinsk Reservoir**. Navigation buffs might be interested to note that from here to St. Petersburg white and red navigational buoys are employed, while from here to Moscow black and red buoys are used. If you don't know which color designates left and which designates right then you don't care about all this anyway.

[KM 533-43] About the city of **Cherepovets** one Soviet guidebook offers: "The abundance of loading cranes and the crowd of cargo ships along the port speak eloquently for the successful enterprises of the city." In translation, it means that this city of 300,000 people is a sprawling industrial setting, a declared environmental disaster area, and one profoundly ugly place. They've been building boats here since 1861, today concentrating mostly on tugboats and barges. The main industry, however, is metallurgy, initiated here after WWII. More than 100 different metals are extracted and forged beneath those mighty smokestacks. According to local literature, the city's second biggest industrial enterprise is a chemical plant "which uses the by-products of the metal plant." Maybe that explains the strange, grayish soot covering all the shrubs and buildings downtown.

The only thing worth scrutinizing around here is the **October Bridge**, a unique center-suspension construction spanning the Sheksna. The bridge stretches for over a kilometer, weighs more than 7,000 tons, and reaches 85 meters above the water. It is certainly the only one of its kind you will see on the journey.

[KM 549 sb] You might see timber awaiting transport on a pier in front of the village of **Lapach**.

[KM 552 sb] This is a little-used military docking area for barges carrying submarines between the Caspian and Baltic seas. Okay, we've never actually seen one, but it sounds kind of thrilling and it might even be true.

[KM 552-68] Along this twisting stretch of river you can see an island or two, a few wooden piers, several villages, and a handful of *dachas*. You might notice metal roofing on many of the dwellings—it's a consequence of the proximity to Cherepovets, a metallurgical center.

[KM 569 p] The ship cruises under a railway bridge close to the mouth of the **Konoma River**. On the bank lies a settlement of *dachas*.

[KM 584 p] The remains of an old wooden lock of the Mariinskaya Canal System can be seen near the village of **Sudbitsy**.

[KM 591-6 sb] The city of **Sheksna** originated in 1905 as a settlement surrounding a railway junction. It gained prominence with the construction of the neighboring hydroplant and today thrives on various industries such as wood-processing, poultry-raising, and butter production. The popular Vologda brand of butter is produced here. But the town's mainstay is growing and processing flax. Incidentally, flax seems to occupy a distinct place in the Russian female soul, as articulated by the extraordinary words of Russian writer Vasily Belov: "Flax for many hundreds of years has been a companion to woman's fate. It is their joy and grief, starting with the boys' diapers, proceeding to the young girls' shawl, and ending finally with a pall." No comment on that doozy. Along the shores of Sheksna's outskirts lie many Soviet-style recreation areas such as pioneer camps and sanatoriums.

[KM 596] The **Sheksna Hydroplant** consists of a hydrostation (uncharacteristically built into the concrete dam) and **Locks # 7 and # 8**. The locks lie side by side and are both operable. Lock # 8 opened in 1992 to alleviate heavy traffic common to this hydroplant. Large passenger ships usually pass through Lock # 8, which measures 310m x 21.5m x 22.8m. The older Lock # 7 measures 265m x 17.5m x 19.7m. The net change in water level in both locks is 13 meters. There is a brief change in slope here, as ships heading to St. Petersburg finally rise, while Moscow-bound ships drop. Incidentally, this hydroplant marks the border between the **Sheksna Reservoir**, with its wide floodwaters, and the **Lower Sheksna River**, with its more natural, narrow and winding course.

[KM 603 sb] Smokestacks in the distance belong to a brick-manufacturing plant.

[KM 603-13] A succession of small villages and farm plots can be seen along both shores of this relatively wide stretch.

[KM 613 p] Many ships make their "green stop" here on the shore below the village of **Irma**. Before partaking of the *shashlik* and wine picnic prepared by your crew, you might venture back along the high-lying dirt road to the **Irdomka River** (a Sheksna tributary) for a swim. Those more sight-oriented might seek out Irma's small church or a nearby monolith to Russian historian N. D. Chechulin, who died here in 1927. The villagers, comprising farmers and *dachniki*, are extremely friendly, and you might be invited to sample some fresh cow milk or beckoned into a home for a *ryumka* of vodka. Beware that many passengers have ended up pretty drunk after these friendly visits. That's why we advise drinking the milk before the vodka. Hanging around the newly built "tourist complex" with its bar, café, and abundant souvenir shopping could keep you out of trouble— plus it's a good place to try Russian beer.

[KM 623 p] In the village of **Gorka** stand the remains of a church, surrounded by trees at the riverfront. On the opposite shore is the village of **Bolshoy Dvor**.

[KM 623-33 sb] Spread along the high banks of this picturesque stretch of reservoir lie too many typical Russian villages to name.

[KM 635-62] Called the **Sizminskiy Floodwaters**, this massive basin resembling a lake formerly was a shallow and winding stretch of the Sheksna River. Teams of horses sometimes were required to pull barges over the shallow rapids. Tree trunks from those days can be seen protruding out of the water.

[KM 662] This point marks the border between the **Upper Sheksna River** and the **Sheksna Reservoir**. Don't look for any markers, as it's more or less an arbitrary division.

[KM 665 sb] Tucked into the reeds near large timber piles hides the first wooden lock of the **Toporninskiy Canal**. The canal is part of the 127 kilometer-long Northern Dvina System. Built in 1825-28 and reconstructed in 1916-21, this network of rivers, canals, and locks was designed to open up navigation to the North from the Volga via the Sheksna. It is primarily used for local transport these days. In the 1970s the central government, looking for something to fill their Five-Year Plan, proposed a major overhaul of the system. The plan called for channeling northern waterways (including the White Sea and Lake Onega) via the Northern Dvina River into the Sheksna and down to the Volga. The idea was to bolster the water supply in southern regions like Kazakhstan. This wacky proposal entailed not only construction of hydropower stations and mass flooding of inhabited areas, but also reversing the flow of several major northern waterways, including lakes as big as Onega. For once reason won out, and the project was scrapped.

[KM 667 sb] Hydrofoils frequently stop at a makeshift pier at the village of **Topornaya**. There used to be a proper pier here serviced by monthly Nizhny Novgorod-St. Petersburg steamships.

[KM 669] Vast timberyards are visible on both shores.

[KM 670-2 p] Perched on a high bank, the settlement of **Ivanov Bor** ("Ivan's Grove") is a jewel to behold, with grand wooden homes, neat plots of land, and tidy riverfront potato patches.

[KM 673 sb] Mounds of concrete mix lie on barges docked along the shore. The mixing takes place in the neighboring green and white structures.

[KM 683] The rustic Resurrection Convent at the river's edge signals your arrival at the village of **Goritsy**. Many ships "lay to" here while their passengers are taken by bus to tour the Monastery of St. Kyrill of the White Lake in the neighboring village of Kirillov.

[KM 687] Just outside Goritsy, the ship sails between two islands, **Gora Gorodok** and **Gora Nikitskaya**. These are names for mountains, which these islands used to be before the Sheksna was flooded.

[KM 687-96] Like many areas along the Sheksna, this is a stretch of flooded forest caused by hydroplant construction.

[KM 703 sb] In the village of **Vognema** stands a quaint church.

[KM 707 p] At **Punkt Chaika**, or "Seagull Point," stands an obelisk marking the entrance to the little-used **White Lake Canal**. The obelisk also marks the halfway point of your journey.

[KM 713] The gloomy, deciduous forests on both banks and the long pontoon bridge (submerged when ships pass) attracted the eye of renowned Russian director Vasily Shukshin, who filmed the Russian classic *Krasnaya Ryabina* ("*Red Rowan Tree*") here.

[KM 714 sb] Always a favorite photo-opportunity, the flooded **Krokhino Church** marks the source of the **Upper**

Sheksna River. The 19th century structure, officially called Nativity Church, stands as a lone symbol of an ancient past. In the 15th century Prince Gleb of Belozersk took shelter here during a White Lake storm and ordered a church built in appreciation of the haven. A few years later he added an entire monastery to the church, this time out of gratitude for his blind 3 year-old son miraculously gaining eyesight. The monastery stood here for more than 500 years. The village of Krokhino itself is thought to have been founded here in 1673 and thrived as an important White Lake port. When the White Lake Canal opened in 1846, ships began bypassing Krokhino. The city entered into decline and the monastery suffered neglect. The technologically gung-ho Soviets finally obliterated the place in the 1960s, flooding it to facilitate the construction of the Sheksna hydroplants. Sigh.

(KM 528 – 714)
ALONG THE VOLGA-BALTIC CANAL:
↟ SHEKSNA RIVER AND RESERVOIR ↟

WHITE LAKE

[KM 714-59] Traversing the **White Lake** should take only about two hours. Although this naturally formed lake is quite large (1,380 square kilometers), it is still technically considered part of the Volga-Baltic Canal. There is not much to point out here, as ships tend to cut directly across the middle of the lake. On the southern shore, near the source of the Sheksna, lies the ancient city of **Belozersk**, visible at some distance. Ever since the 8th century there have been settlements in the Belozersk region. The present day city is situated about 10 kilometers from the original city of Beloozero, which was wiped out by bubonic plague in the 14th century. (Those who survived wisely put a little distance between their old city and their new one.) With binoculars you should be able to pick out a couple of churches. They are likely the Assumption Church, built by the order of Ivan the Terrible in 1553, and the Transfiguration Cathedral, built a little later by order of Ivan's son Tsar Fyodor. (Actually, it's doubtful that Fyodor gave the order, as he was pretty feeble-minded and left the ruling of the country to Boris Godunov.) During the 19th century Belozersk was one of Russia's main lace-weaving centers. Today the city, with over 50 architectural monuments, serves as home port to numerous ships and hydrofoils and is a major timber and fish distribution center.

(KM 714-59)
⬆ WHITE LAKE ⬆

ALONG THE VOLGA-BALTIC CANAL:
WATER DIVISION CANAL & KOVZHA RIVER
(KM 759 – 855)

[KM 759] The **White Lake** and the **Kovzha River** meet at the Kovzha's swollen estuary.

[KM 761 sb] A 200 year-old friend to navigators, the stone Purification Church can be seen on a small island. The island was part of the old village of **Kovzha** (you're sailing over the rest of it), where the St. Nicholas Monastery once stood. Along with 220 other villages, Kovzha was intentionally flooded as part of the upriver canal construction. Of the mass displacement that resulted, one Soviet guidebook offers in a chit-chatty way: "... it was taken by the [tens of thousands of] people as a personal tragedy."

[KM 765 p] With binoculars and a knowledge of Russian you can read the text on a soiled white obelisk protruding out of the water marking the entrance to the narrow **White Lake Canal**. The canal allows small crafts to bypass the White Lake.

[KM 772 sb] The Kovzha spills over into the forest at the mouths of the **Kema** and **Sholopast** rivers. Flooding along the opposite bank is caused by the mouth of the **Shola River**. All of these estuaries may be too far back in the woods to see.

[KM 772-6] Navigators will be on the lookout for floating wood around here, as this is a flooded forest area.

[KM 781 p] At a bend in the river one of Kovzha's tributaries, the **Kitla River**, opens its 600 meter-wide mouth.

[KM 781-91] This stretch of river is welcomed by navigators, as it was recently widened and deepened. It is also a picturesque area with forested banks and lots of small tributaries (whose names are too tongue-twisting to mention) feeding the Kovzha.

[KM 791 p] The village of **Koordyug**, marked by a sign on a dilapidated wooden dock, consists of a smattering of wooden houses. It is situated adjacent to a lumberyard on the shore of a small bay at the mouth of the **Solonka River**. Koordyug was formerly a wood-chopping colony for prisoners—probably during tsarist times, but one never knows.

[KM 802 p] On the shore in a vast clearing stands a landmark well known to navigators. Called the "lonely tree," it's, well, a lonely tree. At last sighting, though, it was being kept company by an old broken-down bus. This is a rather shallow and rocky segment called **Konstantinovskiye Porogi**, or "Konstantin's Rapids." The area is significant because here the canal joins the old Kovzha riverbed, thus marking the beginning or the end (depending on your direction) of the elusive **Kovzha River**.

[KM 818 p] An extremely decrepit yet nonetheless elegant wooden church hides behind the trees.

[KM 823 sb] Bordering the town of Annenskiy Most, a vast riverside lumberyard sports all the tools of the trade—mills, cranes, barges, and astoundingly large piles of timber.

[KM 824] The rather desolate albeit ancient settlement of **Annenskiy Most** is sprinkled on both sides of the river. It's a timber transport center, so you'll likely see rafts and barges to the left of the small river terminal. Naturally you'll also see plenty of wooden dwellings. The two sides of town are connected by a rope-drawn ferry-raft, which you won't see, as it will be submerged to allow the ship to pass.

[KM 838 p] The village of **Rubezh**, meaning "Border," is named such because it lies on the watershed of the Baltic and Volga water basins. Elevation here is estimated at 118.5 meters. During the early 1800s a hospital for laborers working on the Mariinskaya System was here. Scurvy seemed to be the favorite malady of most patients.

[KM 838-855] The ship glides along a narrow stretch of canal (50-100 meters across) on which the maximum speed limit is 12 kilometers per hour. Were crafts to clip along any faster, their wakes would cause increased erosion to the clay banks, which at last check were being fortified in places.

(KM 759 – 855)

ALONG THE VOLGA-BALTIC CANAL:
♠ WATER DIVISION CANAL & KOVZHA RIVER ♠

ALONG THE VOLGA-BALTIC CANAL:
VYTEGRA CANAL AND RESERVOIRS
(KM 855 – 93)

[KM 855] Lock # 6 at the **Pakhomovskiy Hydroplant** is the first or last lock (depending on your direction) of the Volga-Baltic Canal's northern slope. When the lock is full, the ship is 80 meters above Lake Onega and 116 meters above St. Petersburg. The net change in water level here is 16.25 meters. St. Petersburg-bound ships drop; Moscow-bound ships rise. The dimensions of the lock are 264m x 17.7m x 23.5 m. Locking enthusiasts might be interested to know that locks along this canal utilize chambers that are filled and drained through gills at the upper gate rather than through underwater galleries.

[KM 855-61 sb] Between Lock # 5 and # 6 the ship cruises the **Novinkinskoye Reservoir**. The main settlement seen is the ancient village of **Devyatiny**. Its five-domed, wooden Assumption Church, built in 1770, offers a fine example of the striking northern architecture featured most prominently on Kizhi Island. The church formerly contained rare 16th century icons, one of which is now displayed in St. Petersburg's Russian Museum. While the Mariinskaya System was in use, the folks of Devyatiny made a living by transporting ship passengers to the nearby city of Vytegra on horseback. Seems it took so long for ships to pass through those old wooden locks that some passengers just got off and saddled up. Others went ashore and simply walked, picking mushrooms and berries along the way, no doubt. The settlement has grown quite a bit over the last few decades, as families from surrounding, low-lying areas moved here when hydroplant construction flooded their villages.

[KM 861-4] The **Novinkinskiy Hydroplant** consists of three separate locks: **Lock # 3, Lock # 4**, and **Lock # 5**. The combined net change in water level here is 38 meters. St. Petersburg-bound ships drop; Moscow-bound ships rise. Give or take a few centimeters, each lock measures the same: 264m x 17.8m x 19.4m. Those aboard ships heading to Moscow might be interested to know that their approach to Lock # 3 is well known to navigators because it is the only place on the canal where the ship's captain is required to take the helm personally. Somebody go and wake that guy!

[KM 864-9] This body of water is the **Belousovskoye Reservoir**. Keep your eyes out for the village of **Belousovo**, which means "White Mustache" in Russian. (Who knows why it's named that.) On the opposite shore is a WWII memorial statue of a woman supporting a young girl—a sincere nod to the wartime roles played by women.

[KM 869] **Lock # 2** at the **Belousovskiy Hydroplant** was opened along with Lock # 1 in 1961. The net change in water level here is 12.75 meters. St. Petersburg-bound ships drop; Moscow-bound ships rise. The lock's dimensions are 270m x 17.7m x 19.4m.

[KM 871 sb] The wooden houses along a peninsula belong to the village of **Ankhimovo**. You also can see the deteriorating Church of Our Savior (1780) with only one cupola remaining on its five drums. To the left of the church stand a chapel and sepulcher of a 19th century Vytegra merchant. Although telling stories about things that are no longer here isn't exactly fair, it should be mentioned that between the church and the chapel formerly stood the multi-domed, multi-tiered, wooden Intercession Church, conspicuously similar to the breathtaking Transfiguration Cathedral on Kizhi Island. The Intercession Church, built in 1708, was rumored to have been created by the same ax-wielding stud who then built Kizhi's architectural wonder six years later. The one here, unfortunately, burned to the ground in 1963.

[KM 879 sb] Boats sailing on a hidden canal appear to be cutting through the trees as you pass through the city of **Vytegra**. The cupolas in the distance belong to the Purification Cathedral, perched atop Red Hill and built in 1869 to commemorate the city's centennial. As early as the 15th century, though, settlements here engaged in transporting goods over land from Lake Onega to the Kovzha River. (That would be before the canal.) During the first half of the 19th century, Vytegra (Finno-Ugric for "Lake Water") became a bustling provincial center, as it was a primary port along the newly augmented Mariinskaya System. During the second half of the century, a railway was built, the Mariinskaya System declined, and so did the city. Evidently the decline was rather severe. A contemporary observer wrote in 1860: "I have never seen a place more lifeless and sad than Vytegra, which combines all the inconveniences of a small and unorganized town with the deathliness of a village without agricultural activity." It did, however, have all the makings for a splendid place of exile, hosting one of Lenin's co-conspirators, A. D. Tsurupa, in 1903. The city retained some of its past importance when the bordering Vytegra Hydroplant opened in the 1960s. Those passengers aboard ships that stop in Vytegra for a visit—there are a few that do!—will learn all this and more while touring the amusing exhibit located inside the Purification Cathedral. (Placing things like museums in churches was a favorite practice of the communists.) The attentive visitor will notice the authentic Soviet organization of the exhibit—enjoy, as these kinds of places are getting rarer and rarer.

[KM 880] Ships pass through **Lock # 1** at the **Vytegra Hydroplant**, which opened in 1964. The net change in water level here is 13.25 meters. St. Petersburg-bound ships drop; Moscow-bound ships rise. The lock's dimensions are 270m x 17.8m x 19.25m. Constructing it was quite toilful, requiring the excavation of 2 million cubic meters of earth and the laying of 100,000 cubic meters of concrete. The entire chamber of the lock, including its five meter-thick bottom, was assembled on land beside the old wooden Mariinskaya lock it eventually replaced. In town the old wooden lock is on display along with the old lock station.

[KM 882 sb] The town of **Kirpichniy Zavod** is named after a brick plant located here. In addition to timber piles galore, there also is a fishery here where Lake Onega fishermen deliver their catch.

[KM 888 p] The entrance to the **Onega Canal** can be seen. There is a sign marking the point, but unless you can decipher Old Slavonic script you won't be able to read it.

[KM 893] The waters of **Lake Onega** officially join those of the **Vytegra Canal**. By the way, the body of water on which the ship now sails (between locks # 1 and # 2) is the **Vytegra Reservoir**, a massive flood basin covering several old locks of the Mariinskaya System, now some 13 meters below the water. Also submerged is a hill called Besednaya Gora, or "Discussion Mountain" (now an island), where Peter the Great once had a little chat with engineers about the possibility of building a canal here. Peter might have been feeling sympathetic toward the local "barge men" whose job was to pull ships over land from one lock to another using ropes. More likely, Peter was just frustrated by the inefficiency of the operation.

(KM 855 – 93)

ALONG THE VOLGA-BALTIC CANAL:
⬆ VYTEGRA CANAL AND RESERVOIRS ⬆

LAKE ONEGA
(KM 893-950)

[KM 893-950] Most ships don't actually sail along this 57 kilometer stretch of the southern part of **Lake Onega**; the distance is only noted here to preserve the kilometer tally. Instead, they travel approximately 150 kilometers to the lake's northwestern shores to the Karelian capital of **Petrozavodsk**, then cut across the lake for 55 kilometers to visit **Kizhi Island** (or vice-versa). Finally, you head south again for about 150 kilometers to exit the lake and continue your river journey. The net result of all this is some excellent sightseeing and about 300 extra kilometers to your overall total.

(KM 893-950)
↑ LAKE ONEGA ↑

SVIR RIVER
(KM 950 – 1166)

[KM 950] The town of **Voznesenye** is named after the Ascension Monastery, which stood here for some 200 years after its founding in the 16th century. With the opening of the Onega Canal in the 19th century, the town grew substantially, now occupying both banks of the river. One bank presents an industrial face; the other maintains a relatively provincial character, with wooden dwellings of varying styles and wooden walking paths. Residents from the pretty side commute to the ugly side on small boats and ferries. At the Lake Onega end of the town, you pass the entrance to the Onega Canal, a thoroughfare allowing crafts to avoid sometimes turbulent Lake Onega as they travel between the Svir and Kovzha rivers.

[KM 952 sb] You might be able to catch a glimpse of an old WWII pillbox.

[KM 955 sb] The village of **Chashcheruchey**, which means something like "Thicket Stream," can be identified by a railway-serviced pier where river rafts are disassembled. On the opposite shore is the village **Karnavolok** where rafts from northern rivers are reassembled to continue journeying along the Svir.

[KM 957 p] The settlement of **Krasniy Bor**, or "Red Grove," is distinguished by an old, Gogolesque, wooden church which likely dates from the 17th or early 18th century. (What's *Gogolesque*? Read Gogol.)

[KM 961-7 p] A long island called **Ivanko** might be mistaken for the riverbank.

[KM 979 sb] In front of the village of **Gakruchey** stands a pier where passengers used to board monthly ships sailing between Nizhny Novgorod and St. Petersburg.

[KM 982-95] Ships operate under lake navigational conditions while cruising this 117 square kilometer "man-made sea" called the **Ivinskiy Flooded Area**. It is not called a reservoir because it is simply an area that engineers of the Upper Svir Hydroplant decided to flood without fortifications—or regard for the ecology for that matter. Wildlife you might spot around here include duck, woodcock, and white partridge. Log cabins you might spot along the shore are where St. Petersburg hunters drink vodka after shooting the wildlife. Also, in places you might notice fencing protruding a meter or so out of the water. It is designed to catch islands of peat which tend to float around willy-nilly creating a nuisance for ship navigators and lock operators.

[KM 995-1026] Except for an occasional high-lying settlement, this is a pretty uninhabited stretch of river due to the flooding of villages that resulted from the construction of the Upper Svir Hydroplant. Ah, the triumphs of modern technology.

[KM 1026-8] Passing the village of **Myatusovo**, similar to Khevronino.

[KM 1031-3 sb] The village on the bank is **Khevronino**, approximately 500 years old. Most of its inhabitants work in quarries or raise cattle. Many of the houses along the shores are over one hundred years old and are fine examples of typical architecture of the Russian North, with log foundations and sharply pitched roofs to facilitate snow runoff. If some of the dwellings look unusually large, it is due to the tradition of newlywed couples building their homes to adjoin those of their parents. Sure, the front doors may be on opposite sides of the house, but it still seems like a potentially volatile arrangement. Houses' roofs often extend over the barn and cattle shed so that farming duties can be performed during wintertime without venturing outside. A potentially stinky arrangement?

[KM 1034] As the banks become taller and more striking, the river bends sharply at an area called **Medvedyets Kolyeno**, a Russian derivative meaning "Bear's Knee."

[KM 1040] The **Upper Svir Lock (Hydroplant)** is set amidst the shipyards, lumberyards, and cargo ports of Podporozhye. There are several nifty sights in and around this lock. On the outside of the upper towers, bas-relief panels depict scenes of the lock's construction. Crowning the lower towers are plaster hammer-and-sickle sculptures on which stand iron replicas of various riverships. Four different types of vessels, representing the history of river travel, are depicted: sailboat, galley, steamship, and modern motorship. If your ship ties up in the very middle of the lock chamber, you'll be face to face with a white monolith featuring a portrait of Lenin. The prominent inscription below the portrait reads, "Lenin lived, Lenin lives, Lenin will live!" While you snicker, here is some technical information on the lock: The net change in water level here is 24 meters. St. Petersburg-bound ships drop; Moscow-bound ships rise. The lock's dimensions are 281m x 21.5m x 30.5m. Construction of the plant started in 1932, was interrupted by the war, and finally completed in 1951.

[KM 1040-7] During WWII, **Podporozhye**, now spread out on both banks of the river, was just a small village. It was occupied by the Germans for three years, but boasted some spectacular war heroes. (Pay attention, all you blood-and-guts enthusiasts.) Two of them, Anna Lisitzina, age 19, and Mariya Melentyeva, age 17, came into possession of enemy documents and set out to deliver them to Soviet headquarters in Karelia, to the north. Crossing the Svir, Anna drowned from cramps, biting her own arm to muffle her screams. Mariya made it across and walked through the thick Karelian forest without food for days. She finally reached headquarters and turned over the documents. Upon returning home to Podporozhye, she was promptly killed by

German troops. Another local hero, Valeriya Gnarovskaya, age 19, was a nurse who flung her grenade-wrapped body beneath an enemy tank on the battlefield. Needless to say, there are quite a few memorials standing in the town. War stories aside, the village of Podporozhye became a major settlement fifty years ago during the construction of the Upper Svir Hydroplant. Today the settlement is an industrial center and headquarters to Svir River navigational dispatchers.

[KM 1047] The river is pretty narrow here (about 100 meters across) and the current is fairly swift. Ships cruise under a steel bridge which can be raised if the water level is too high for safe passage.

[KM 1050-2 sb] The town of **Nikolskiy** was founded by Peter the Great, who "settled" Moscow Germans here for the purpose of casting chains and anchors for his wooden ships being built down the river at Lodeinoye Pole. After that project was concluded, the place was pretty dismal and stagnant all the way up to 1945, when a shipyard was built. It now produces motorboats, docks, and cargo cranes.

[KM 1055 sb] The town of **Vazhiny** administrates all lumber yards along the Svir. A recently completed, rail-connected cargo port on the town's outskirts functions as an important commerce junction. You might see Volga riverboats waiting to unload their wares into train cars destined for St. Petersburg or Murmansk.

[KM 1057 sb] The ship hugs the bank at the mouth of the **Vazhinka River** along which the ancient practice of timber-floating still goes on.

[KM 1064 sb] The town of **Uslanka** was well known for its iron foundry until the plant was flooded when the river was dammed. Now the settlement is pretty sleepy and considerably smaller than it once was.

[KM 1067-9] Two docks, on which are often piled coal and sand, protrude from the dense forest into this very narrow stretch. Tricky for navigators, this is a "one-way" section of river.

[KM 1071-86] This forest-lined stretch of river is actually a reservoir formed by the dam of the Lower Svir Hydroplant. Rivers **Mondraga** and **Sara** enter along the way; their mouths make for popular local recreation areas.

[KM 1086 p] The riverside settlement of **Svirstroy**, sprinkled with *dachas*, is where builders of the Lower Svir Hydroplant resided. Some ships make a quick "green stop" here, allowing passengers to stretch their legs on land.

[KM 1087] The ship enters the **Lower Svir Lock (Hydroplant)**. There is an amusing anecdote (taken from Soviet literature) connected with the construction of this hydroplant. Intent on harnessing the Svir's waters in compliance with Lenin's 1920 State Plan for the Electrization of Russia, Soviet engineers invited their American counterparts for feasibility consultations. The Americans advised against building a dam and lock at this location due to soft clay and sand beneath the earth's surface. Putting it nicely, they deemed the project technologically adventurous, concluding that a dam here would sooner or later fall. Unimpressed with the American evaluation, the chief Soviet engineer proclaimed, "The station will be built, and it will work for socialism!" So in spring 1927, top Communist Party officials Kirov and Kalinin themselves came here to lay the first stones. The facility opened in 1933 and operated without incident for the next ten years. Then it fell, but not of its own accord. The Soviet Army blew up the lock's gates during WWII to flood advancing German troops. After the war, the lock was rebuilt and has been working—albeit not entirely for socialism—ever since.

The net change in water level here is 12.1 meters. The

lock's dimensions are 198m x 21.5m x 20.4m. Ships coming from St. Petersburg rise (and, oh yes, welcome to the first lock of your journey; but don't get too excited, there will be plenty more). Ships from Moscow drop (and that's all she wrote, lockwise, for your journey).

[KM 1096 p] A small settlement named **Yanega** lies where a river of the same name joins the Svir. On the opposite shore are scattered a few white houses and a two-story building with narrow windows, which houses the administration of the Svirskiy fish breeding grounds. Its purpose is to keep the Svir and its tributaries stocked with salmon and trout, as the dam of the Lower Svir Hydroplant messes up the fishes' natural spawning routes. Whether or not the grounds are still operable is difficult to determine.

[KM 1098] The ship passes under the middle section of the **Lodeinopolskiy Bridge**.

[KM 1099-104 p] The ship cruises by the historical town of **Lodeinoye Pole**, spread out on a high bank. The town's name means "Boat Yard," for it was here that Peter the Great instituted a large shipyard in 1702. Peter summoned his old Dutch shipbuilding buddies, along with craftsmen from around Russia, to build his wooden sailing fleet. Peter's right-hand man, Alexander Menshikov, personally supervised the works, and Peter himself visited frequently to lend an expert hand. Operable well into the 19th century, the shipyard produced some 450 vessels out of local timber. After the yard closed, Lodeinoye Pole dwindled until the 1930s, at which time construction of the nearby Lower Svir Hydroplant renewed the town's importance. During WWII the settlement had the misfortune of lying at the front of Soviet defense lines and was pretty much destroyed. On the river bank in the midst of a cemetery (partially eclipsed by trees) stands a commemorative statue of a soldier proudly holding a shield.

[KM 1105 p] On the shore you should see substantial amounts of timber (or an appalling number of dead trees, depending on your point of view) awaiting river transport.

[KM 1121] A fairly sizable island called **Konev**, or "Horse Island," will be passed in this vicinity. It is densely forested and surrounded by marshland.

[KM 1127 sb] Where the **Segazha River** joins the Svir you might see a few houses; they constitute the villages **Gorka** and **Kofkinitsa**.

[KM 1131 sb] There is an island around here called **Gneelno**; its name derives from a Russian word applied to dangerous, remote, marshy areas. If you happen to be here in August and the ship doesn't seem to be moving, it's probably been waylaid by fog.

[KM 1131-47] Nothing particularly amusing here, just an austerely serene stretch of narrow river with tall, jagged banks of a reddish hue and abundant pine and fir.

[KM 1152 p] On the right bank of the **River Oyat**, which enters here, lies a row of wooden houses comprising the village of **Sermaksa**, one of the oldest on the Svir. It has a bit of a hardy history: In the 16th century, the Swedes sacked it. In the early 17th century, during the Time of Troubles, one of the False Dmitrys attempted to commandeer the place, but was turned away by ax- and scythe-wielding peasants. During the 18th and 19th centuries, it served as a place of exile for political agitators. In 1907 the agitators couldn't resist agitating some more and organized a massive raftsmen strike. After the 1917 Revolution, Sermaksa played host to a more underhanded form of exile—a massive state farm named after Lenin.

[KM 1159 p] Floating in the mouth of the **Pasha River**, the settlement of **Sviritsa** spreads over eight islands around which the **Novosvirskiy Canal** winds, providing passage for ships and freighters. This important 13th century Novgorod trading port today is home to ship navigators and timber industry workers.

[KM 1159-66] This is roughly the area of the **Svir River** mouth. It is not clearly discernible because of its 700 meter width, which is the result of another river mouth here, that of a major Svir tributary, the **Pasha River**. This entire area, in addition to some 40,000 hectares beyond the shores and along the river itself, is a state natural preserve: home to elk, bear, lynx, and numerous species of water fowl, including frequently seen gray crane. Two of the larger islands passed by the ship are named **Oleniy** and **Leesiy**, or "Deer" and "Fox" islands.

(KM 950 – 1166)
⬆ SVIR RIVER ⬆

LAKE LADOGA
(KM 1166-315)

[KM 1166-315] Ships operate under sea navigational conditions as they cross **Lake Ladoga**. "Sea navigational conditions" may sound threatening, but usually the trip is pretty smooth sailing. Usually. For those of you kilometer-counters whose itineraries include a stop at **Valaam Island** in the northern reaches of the lake, add about 200 extra kilometers to your trip's total. Ships not diverting to Valaam will cross the southern width of the lake (a 149 km stretch), passing by the lighthouse-crowned island of **Sukho** (approximately halfway across the lake), itself a WWII battle monument. In the bay near the mouth of the Svir River passengers on all ships should be able to catch a glimpse of a red and white structure resembling a tall smokestack. This is the lighthouse of **Storozhno**, marking a settlement where, according to lore, a band of 16th century pirates were once so thankful to be saved from a perilous storm that they changed their ways and founded a monastery.

NEVA RIVER
(KM 1315 – 69)

[KM 1315-7 p] There are several major points of interest along this stretch where the **Neva River** joins **Lake Ladoga**. Of greatest interest is the island fortress called *Petrokrepost* by Russians, but known as **Schlüsselburg** to the rest of us. Representing a typical saga of Russian naming and renaming, the island, first fortified in 1323 by Georgiy of Novgorod, was known to the Russians as *Oreshek*, or "little nut," and to the Swedes as *Noteburg*. The two adversaries bickered and killed each other over the thing until 1702, when Peter the Great captured it once and for all and named it *Schlüsselburg*, German for "Key Fortress." In 1944, when German sentiment wasn't real high, the island's name was changed to the Russian *Petrokrepost*, or "Peter's Fortress," and was staunchly defended by the Soviet army for the duration of WWII. Just for kicks, recently it has reverted to the name *Shlisselburg*, a Russified form of the original.

On the mainland is the city of Petrokrepost, or Shlisselburg, or whatever you want to call it. Aside from the massive Nevsky Shipyard, the main visible point of interest is the Baroque Annunciation Cathedral, painted apricot and white yet in rather derelict shape since its closure in 1930. Along with scores of other churches, this one was returned to Orthodox hands in the government's post-*perestroika* rush to religious embrace—or rather, its unloading of a hefty host of neglected historical monuments.

For the 200 or so years between the Northern War and the 1917 Bolshevik Revolution, the Schlüsselburg fortress was used as a prison and execution site for all kinds of nemeses of the tsar, ranging from Peter the Great's first wife to Lenin's brother Alexander. With a reputation that made Alcatraz Island seem like a Sheraton by comparison, the island was converted into a revolutionary museum by the Communists during the 1920s. Today a specialized adventure travel firm can arrange for you to spend two weeks locked in one of the prison's old cells with nothing but a mattress, pen, and paper. They provide meager meals as well as daily psychological check-ups—just in case the ghosts believed to inhabit the thick stone walls begin to get to you. The idea is to "challenge" yourself and/or get in touch with yourself. You actually get a certificate at the end of your self-imposed sentence. The funny thing is that people actually pay money to do this.

A jetty, also on the mainland, marks the entrances to two separate canals. The canal to the right, **Old Ladoga Canal**, was started by the hands of Peter the Great in 1719. The tsar was sick and tired of Svir River-bound vessels capsizing in the rough waters of Lake Ladoga—10,000 crafts went down from 1703 to 1731—and wanted a way to bypass the trouble. The left-side canal, **New Ladoga Canal**, was opened in 1866 to accommodate steamboats and was the main water route to and from the Svir for the next hundred years. It is still used today by light crafts.

[KM 1319 p] As you pass the settlement of **Ugolniy** you might spot large deposits of coal awaiting river transport on the shore.

[KM 1325 p] Where the nine-section **Ladoga Bridge** joins the Neva's south bank look out for a WWII memorial in the form of a genuine Soviet T-34 tank. Inside the bridge itself is a diorama-museum called "The Break of the Siege."

[KM 1330 p] The city of **Kirovsk** can be identified by a hydroelectric plant, smokestacks atop an old gray factory, and a nursery. A statue of the revolutionary figure Kirov may or may not still be standing near the hydroelectric plant. Kirovsk is known as a "regional center," which means that it has a theater, a college, and a department store. Additionally, quite a number of folks in these parts raise cattle and chickens.

[KM 1332 p] On the shore a large granite pillar stands as a monument to the former town of **Arbuzovo**, which was virtually eradicated during WWII along with a substantial number of Soviet troops. Passing ships often sound their horns in memory of the lives lost.

[KM 1336 p] The wooden houses amidst the trees constitute the village of **Lobanovo**, located near the mouth of the **Mga River**.

[KM 1338] The **Kuzminskiy Railway Bridge** (blown up in self-defense by Soviet troops in 1941 and rebuilt in 1954) consists of three segments, one of which should be raised to allow the ship's passage.

[KM 1341 sb] A small island called **Glav Ryba**, or "Fish Central," was once a salmon breeding grounds.

[KM 1344-6 p] The ship sails through the 2 km-long **Ivanovskiye Rapids**. Moscow-bound vessels are given the right-of-way in this bottleneck where the current moves at a rate of 3 meters per second. At the St. Petersburg end of the rapids, the **Tosna River** joins its younger sister, the Neva, at the site of the Otradinsky cargo port and shipyard. Spanning the mouth of the Tosna are two bridges which Soviet troops successfully defended during WWII. A stone obelisk standing in a military cemetery commemorates the effort. On the opposite shore, an even more impressive WWII monument can be seen: a large earthen pyramid with concrete steps called "Nameless Hill" on which Soviet soldiers successfully vowed never to allow a German footprint.

[KM 1353-7 p] The **Ust-Izhora** settlement lies on the Neva's southern bank where the **Izhora River** enters. A church (at last sighting under restoration) stands nearby on the site where on 15 July 1240 Russian hero Alexander Yaroslavovich, prince of Novgorod, ambushed Swedes who were planning to cross the Neva with the nasty idea of capturing the Novgorod lands. For his part in repelling the Swedes, Alexander was bestowed with the name *Nevsky*, meaning "of the Neva." He got all kinds of nice things named after him, including St. Petersburg's Alexander Nevsky Monastery, and even was canonized. Keep your eye out for a commemorative stone the Soviets got around to laying in 1957.

[KM 1364 sb] The settlement along the bank is **Novosaratov** ("New Saratov"), founded in the 18th century by former residents of the Volga city Saratov. On the opposite shore lies a suburb called **Rybatskoye**, or "Fisherman's Village," where the tsar's private fishermen used to reside.

[KM 1367 sb] At the St. Petersburg city line the ship navigates a wide section of river called **Utkina zavod**, or "Duck's Backwater," where passenger ships and barges are docked for repair. A notable green industrial-like structure is a thermal electricity plant called "Red October." One of the first of its kind in the country, this plant alone provided electricity to the city during the WWII blockade of Leningrad. If you can pick out a building on the opposite shore that resembles a steel mill, you are likely viewing a mill called Bolshevik, where St. Petersburg's first Marxist proletarian societies were formed.

[KM 1369] Welcome to **St. Petersburg's River Passenger Terminal**, built in 1970. Don't let the drabness of the port worry you; downtown Petersburg presents a welcome contrast. Really.

(KM 1315 – 1369)

NEVA RIVER

⬆ THE RIVER ROUTE ⬆

**(begins here for passengers
originating in St. Petersburg)**

PORTS OF CALL

Use this section to learn about the history, population, and sights of each city at which the ship casts anchor. Within each chapter we have also included a sub-section entitled "The Inside Scoop" with tips on how to make the most out of organized shore excursions as well as how to most effectively strike out on your own.

Cities are ordered as visited from Moscow to St. Petersburg.

Metric conversions that may come in handy:

1 meter	= 1.09 yards (3.28 feet)
1 kilometer	= 0.62 miles
1 square kilometer	= 0.39 square miles

MOSCOW

ORIENTATION

Welcome to the capital of the largest country on earth, the onetime seat of an empire and command-post of global politics that is alternately considered to be Asian, European, both, and neither. Almost 850 years old and currently existing amidst rapidly changing political and economic conditions, Moscow presents a dizzying array of the old and new, the alienating and quaint, the shabby and sparkling.

HISTORY

One would expect the founding of Russia's very own Mecca to be well documented, but it is not. The generally accepted version is that Suzdal Prince Yury Dolgoruky (the Long-armed) visited a village atop Borovitsky Hill (the sight of the present Kremlin) in 1147 and decided it had all the makings of a future metropolis. He returned in 1156 to build a wooden fortress, and Moscow was born.

Along with Yaroslavl, Kostroma, and the rest of the Vladimir-Suzdal realm, Moscow was sacked by Mongol-Tatars in 1237-38. It rebounded quickly and became the head of its own principality in 1276 under the rule of its first prince, Daniil. Practically all the principalities of Russia at this time were vassals of the Mongol yoke, which allowed the princedoms relative independence so long as they functioned as dutiful tax-collecting agencies. As his name would suggest, Prince Ivan I the Moneybags was quite adept at the game and was given the title of Grand Prince of Muscovy in 1328. Soon thereafter Muscovy absorbed the Vladimir and Suzdal principalities on its way to becoming the center of the empire for the next 300 years.

Although the Mongols burned Moscow down in 1382 as a little revenge for their defeat by Dmitry Donskoy at Kulikovo two years earlier, their empire fell into enough disarray by the 15th century for Ivan III (the Great) to shirk

Mongol domination and establish Moscow as the official capital of the Russian lands. In order to create a capital so awe-inspiring that "reality would embody fantasy on an unearthly scale," Ivan invited Pskov and Italian architects to rebuild the old wooden kremlin in stone. By 1495 they had completed the walls and towers. Ivan must have been amazed at the "New Constantinople" that had been created by his Russo-Italian team. New cathedrals were commissioned, squares laid, and decorative gardens planted throughout the city. Moscow became the beautiful "big village" that it is patronizingly referred to today by non-Muscovites.

Ivan the Great's grandson Ivan IV (the Terrible) was born in the Kremlin and had himself crowned tsar (the first to assume the title) within its walls at age sixteen. Ivan married seven times, killed off most of his boyars, and slew his own eldest son in a fit of rage, but saved historical face by "gathering the Russian lands." Although it was his grandfather who united most of the principalities, it was Ivan IV who captured the Golden Horde khanates of Kazan and Astrakhan, thereby claiming the entire Volga region for Russia. He was so proud of conquering once mighty Kazan he commemorated the feat by commissioning the construction of stupendous St. Basil's Cathedral (the one in front of which Western newscasters always stand when broadcasting from Moscow).

The Polish army occupied Moscow in 1610-12, the peak of the Time of Troubles. They were driven out by a Volga-region army led by a mayor named Minin and a prince named Pozharsky, whose bronze likenesses today stand in front of St. Basil's Cathedral. Young boyar Michael Romanov emerged from the anarchy to take the throne, kicking off a dynasty that was to turn its back on Moscow for much of its 300 years of reign by ruling from St. Petersburg, a place that was still only a swamp at the time of Michael's death in 1645.

Moscow's fall from grace began with the rule of Peter the Great (1696-1725). The sedulous young tsar resented Moscow for being too Russian. He thought the country would be more easily Westernized from the Gulf of Finland, which is where he began building his new capital, St. Petersburg. Peter's "window on the West" officially wrested the governing powers from Moscow in 1712. Because Peter compelled the country's important figures to inhabit the new capital, it began to assume a cosmopolitan air while Moscow took a humbling back seat.

Napoleon, a romantic sort who didn't care if Moscow was no longer the capital, focused his campaign of 1812 on the capture of the ancient city, a feat he pulled off fairly easily, notwithstanding some admirable Russian resistance at Borodino. Spending his first gleeful night in the Kremlin, the French commander went to sleep thinking his war won. Soon, however, he began to wonder why no declaration of Russian capitulation was arriving. He realized that the entire city population had simply left him and his troops to brave the upcoming Moscow winter on their own. Never having before faced such tactics, which sort of took the fun out of the conquering business, he hastily retreated, burning down most of the city but failing to topple the mighty Kremlin itself.

Even Tolstoy, who wrote that "it would be difficult to explain what caused the Russians, after the departure of the French in 1812, to throng to the place that had been known as Moscow," was amazed by the alacrity with which the city recovered. Within a year the population exceeded what it had been in 1812. By the end of the century it had exceeded one million. The revival, unfortunately, was fostered primarily by large-scale industrial expansion. Manufacturing enterprises spread out along the Moscow River embankment. The city's beloved gardens gave way to smoke-belching factories; nine thousand gardens dwindled to a few hundred. Shabby suburbs appeared to house the influx of workers. Rather than being preserved as a living chronicle of Russian history, the city was transformed into the country's biggest industrial center.

The Bolsheviks overcame savage street fighting in October 1917 to capture the Kremlin en route to achieving socialist revolution. In March 1918, with Soviet power declared across the country, Lenin and his Bolsheviks brought the capital back to Moscow. The party of the working class took up its operations within the ancient walls of the historical seat of royalty. "Necessary dictatorship" was established as a temporary transitional measure. It became, however, a permanent way of governing.

With characteristic politeness, *Fodor's* comments on the post-Lenin period thus: "There followed years of much suffering and hardship..." To be somewhat less oblique, the city was virtually raped by irresponsible leaders, most notably a mustachioed monster named Josef Stalin.

Using an army of cost-efficient labor (GULAG prisoners) and liberal amounts of TNT, the notorious champion of "progress" went about redesigning the capital so that it would reflect the "triumphant march of socialism." As outlined in the General Plan for the Reconstruction of Moscow, thousands of historical and architectural monuments were blown up, including such gems as the Church of Christ the Savior (totally rebuilt in 1997). Streets were straightened and widened, neighborhoods demolished, and seven ominous "Stalinist Gothic" skyscrapers sprung up around the Garden Ring. By the time of Stalin's death in 1953, a full half of Moscow's historical and architectural monuments had been turned into dust. The new alienating city layout, designed to flout pomp, not only drained the ancient capital of charm and romance, but substantially cleansed it of traditional Russian character. It was a feat that likely would have made Peter the Great proud.

During the Khrushchev years, Moscow's outskirts were littered with *khrushchevky*, hastily built residential projects resembling concrete blocks and containing cramped flats. The Brezhnev years were characterized by stagnation, except for a brief period in 1980, when in preparation for the Olympic Games, Moscow gained a few stadiums and hotels and swept its dirt under the carpet for a spell. Privatization sparked by Mikhail Gorbachev's *perestroika* resulted in the renovation of some world-class hotels and the appearance of swanky restaurants, clubs, and casinos which go in and out of business depending on their popularity and Mafia protection. Since Boris Yeltsin's rise to power, Moscow has increasingly come to resemble a bustling Eurasian metropolis, as omnipresent kiosks and street traders stake their claim to Russia's furious fledgling capitalism.

ABOUT THE CITY

That first-time visitors as well as lifelong Muscovites so easily overlook evidence of the city's rocky history is not surprising, so extraordinary and diverse are Moscow's intrinsic attributes. Ascribing the city's uncanny allure to its having one foot in Asia and one in Europe is, frankly, an overused cop-out. Moscow simply is Moscow. Although, while standing on Teatralnaya Ploshchad surrounded by the Classical presence of the Bolshoy Theater, the Art Deco touches of the Metropol Hotel, and the Byzantine imposition of the distant Kremlin towers, one certainly feels as if amidst a fairy tale whose origins are elusive.

In any Russian city the word *tsentr* (center) is used to denote the downtown heart; throughout the country at large, *tsentr* also refers to Moscow itself, the center of everything in Russia. Political coups, theatrical debuts, scientific revelations, and fashion trends all originate in the country's capital. With something like 2,500 historical and architectural monuments, 70 museums, 125 cinemas, 50 theaters, 4,500 libraries, 540 higher educational and research institutions, including the oldest university in the country, and a labyrinth of back streets and secluded neighborhoods, the city requires a lifetime to fully explore. Summer, when the temperature reaches into the twenties (centigrade), is probably the optimal time to become acquainted with the city; yet there is something about the snow-covered Kremlin cupolas that almost justifies a visit during the below-freezing winter months.

The populace of Russia's largest city is engaged in a variety of industries, including metalworking, oil refining, automobile manufacturing, chemical, wood, and paper processing, film production, tourism, and lately, good old fashioned wholesale/retail. At last count, Moscow's population was around nine million people, who consume an average of two million bottles of vodka per day.

SIGHTS

You'll hear the exclamation "*Oy!*" a lot in Russia—whenever someone stubs a toe, nearly runs into a car, or faces a task of daunting proportions. When it comes to outlining all the possible sights in Moscow, the authors of this humble river cruise companion take the liberty of pronouncing a big "*Oy!*" and kindly referring you to any of the comprehensive city guidebooks found here or abroad. Below, however, we introduce you to the major sights usually covered by ships' shore excursions. Additionally, see "The Inside Scoop" section for further sightseeing suggestions.

The Kremlin

> Towers of every form, round, square, and with pointed roofs, belfries, donjons, turrets, spires, sentry boxes upon minarets, steeples of every height, style and colour, palaces, domes, watchtowers, walls, embattlemented and pierced with loopholes, ramparts, fortifications of every species, whimsical inventions, incompre-

> hensible devices, chiosks by the sides of cathe-
> drals... (sic)

Such was the initial impression of the Moscow Kremlin upon the rather disparaging consciousness of the Marquis de Custine, who toured Russia in 1839. Although the function of several of the Kremlin's structures may have changed a few times since then, the presence of the most breathtaking citadel on earth has not. The present Kremlin is the legacy of Ivan the Great, who rebuilt a pre-existing fortress at the end of the 15th century. "But," states Custine, "if this place was not built by Ivan the Terrible, it was built for him." The allusion is to the despotism that Custine ascribed to the awesome architecture itself. Indeed, it was from within the Kremlin walls that Ivan the Terrible fashioned his tyranny, Napoleon watched the city burn, Lenin redirected his revolution toward dictatorship, Stalin barked his genocidal commands, and Brezhnev snored while his country fell decades behind the West.

Don't let its history intimidate you; the only treachery facing the modern day visitor to the Kremlin is posed by swarming summer tour groups. The crowds are certainly worth bearing, though, for the various structures within the Kremlin comprise the historical heart and soul of Russia.

The white limestone **Assumption Cathedral**, its five gilded cupolas glittering atop narrow drums, stood for centuries as the national shrine of Russia. Tsars were coronated and patriarchs crowned in front of its altar. Even after the seat of the monarchy was moved to St. Petersburg, new sovereigns, including the last tsar, doomed Nicholas II, journeyed to Moscow to commence their reign officially. Don't think this wasn't a venerated tradition—Empress Elizabeth used up 800 horses to pull her carriage here from St. Petersburg in 1741. Of the cathedral's interior, Custine, who was perhaps a bit too biased toward the Gothic likes of Chartres to be objective, remarked, "The church is nearly square, very lofty, and so small that on walking in it you feel as if in a dungeon." (Was it mentioned he was rather disparaging?) Somewhere in the church (doubtlessly somewhere inaccessible) is a collection of holy relics, allegedly including one of the nails driven through Jesus of Nazareth's wrists. Standing on the oldest square in Moscow, the cathedral was built in 1475 in a Byzantine style with Renaissance touches. Napoleon used the church as a horse stable and some of its icons for firewood while he graced the Kremlin with his presence in 1812.

The **Annunciation Cathedral**, built in the late 1500s, served for centuries as personal shrine for the tsars. These days it boasts an unequaled collection of significant icons, many rendered by Theophanes the Greek, considered one of the finest of all icon painters. Hence, if Moscow is the beginning of your trip, here is your *de rigueur* introduction to Orthodox icons, of which you will be seeing a plethora more. If your trip terminates in Moscow, this is probably the *coup de grâce* for you and icons. The cathedral was originally a simple, three-domed affair, but Ivan the Terrible added six more cupolas, four chapels, and a dazzling gilded roof. He also commissioned the construction of a side entrance for his personal use, as poor Ivan was forbidden by the patriarch to use the main entrance. (It had something to do with Ivan's having too many wives.)

Across from the Annunciation Cathedral stands the five-domed **Archangel Michael Cathedral**, built in 1505-08. The floor space inside is monopolized by sarcophagi, but don't be put out by the inconvenience—they contain the remains of practically every Russian tsar up to the reign of Peter the Great. If you can't decipher Old Slavonic script, you might have a hard time identifying who is who. Even if you can read Old Slavonic, you unfortunately won't be able to locate Ivan the Terrible's tomb, which rests behind the iconostasis. Those who have already visited the site of the murder of Ivan's son Dmitry in Uglich might be interested to know that the young saint is resting more or less peacefully here beneath a painted stone canopy.

At the edge of the Kremlin grounds is Russia's oldest and most fascinating museum, the **State Armory Chamber**. Don't be deceived by the name; there is much, much more here than mere artifacts of war. In fact, the museum could alternatively be called the "Exhibition of Royal Excess." Try not to think about the oppression that has plagued Russian people throughout the ages as you saunter past Boris Godunov's throne, encrusted with 2,000 precious stones; Alexey Romanov's throne, adorned with 1,000 diamonds; or Catherine the Great's coronation crown, covered with pearls and 5,000 diamonds. These imperial toys are just the tip of the iceberg. Prepare yourself for gold and silver galore—chalices, bowls, goblets, jewelry—as well as royal vestments, robes, and headdresses. The Armory houses the world's largest collection of carriages, which is displayed in one stupendous room alive with gilded swirls of Baroque and Rococo monsters the likes of which you've never imagined. And then there's always the 189-carat Orlov Diamond that Count Orlov gave to his mistress, Catherine the Great, and then... well, you get the idea. By the way, the fabulous Fabergé eggs are sometimes exhibited here, but they have a tendency to move around, so you'll likely have to ask your guide how to track them down in order to behold their miracles.

Besides the four above-mentioned destinations within the Kremlin, the only other sights your local guide is sure to walk you past are the 40-ton **Tsar Cannon**, the largest cannon in the world (never fired), and the 210-ton **Tsar Bell**, the largest bell in the world (never rung). While pondering what these two monstrosities say about the character of Russian leaders, why not sally on up to the bell for a picture—don't be shy, everybody else is doing it.

Red Square
Probably the most famous square in the world, this is where you really feel like you're in Russia—with good reason, as here is where government decrees were read, tsars' opponents slaughtered, potatoes and vodka bartered, and Soviet leaders dutifully tributed by their subjects on state holidays, in reality sham pageants followed by energetic socializing and drinking. Here also is where young German pilot Mathias Rust cheekily landed his Cessna in 1987, causing the Soviet government a wee bit of embarrassment. You can bet *he* really felt like he was in Russia upon disembarking.

Cobblestone throughout its 70,000 square meter expanse (the stones came from a quarry near Lake Onega), Red Square is bordered by the Kremlin wall, St. Basil's Cathedral, GUM department store, and the multi-gabled, red brick State Historical Museum.

The square is still oriented around the famed **Lenin Mausoleum**, lying in front of the Kremlin wall. Having fallen out of fashion, Lenin is soon to be moved from his honored domicile. The fate of the granite and marble Constructivist mausoleum itself is still unknown, although there has been no shortage of amusing suggestions. Visitors in 1993 were the last to witness the spectacle of the tomb's goose-stepping guards changing every hour, but you can still venture inside to experience the other-worldliness of the mausoleum's dark interior and to contribute to the debate about whether Lenin is real or wax. (He's waxy-real.) Although no one knows where Lenin will ultimately end up, rumor has it that the government is contemplating sending him on a world tour to raise badly needed hard currency. They better hurry, though, as poor Lenin reportedly shrinks a few centimeters each year. On a related side note, Russian scientists recently took the liberty of performing an autopsy on the formerly revered ruler's brain, determining that the organ's capacity is that of an average Ivan.

Behind the mausoleum a **mini-cemetery** of sorts stretches along the Kremlin wall. Here are the final resting places of a motley crew of since-disgraced Soviet heroes, some of whose ashes lie in urns within the Kremlin wall. You can pay your respects to the likes of Chernenko, Andropov, Brezhnev, Dzerzhinsky, Kirov, Sverdlov, and the most infamous of all, Stalin, who judging by the abundance of flowers on his slab is still loved despite having systematically exterminated 30 million of his countrymen. More neutral figures honored here include cosmonaut Yury Gagarin, Soviet writer Maxim Gorky, and misguided American journalist John Reed.

What captivates the visitor to Red Square is the orgy of multicolored onion domes that is **St. Basil's Cathedral**. Despite being exploited by travel posters, guidebook covers, and satellite broadcasts, the image of Russia's signature monument somehow transcends itself, captivating the onlooker as if it were never seen before. Considered the embodiment of traditional Russian architecture, the structure actually is a deviation from convention, consisting of nine connected chapels organized on a fairly simple layout. The legend that guides like to tell about Ivan gouging out the eyes of the cathedral's architect to preclude the possibility of Russia ever again having such an architectural *chef-d'œuvre* is horrible in an entertaining way and quite in line with Ivan's reputation, but alas, untrue. The two architects that built the original structure, in fact, went on to add a chapel to it four years after Ivan died.

On the opposite side of the square from the Kremlin wall sprawls the facade (although not containing the entrance) of Russia's largest shopping center, **GUM**. Pronounced "goom," the name constitutes the initials for the Russian words "State Department Store." Designed in 1895 to house 200 trading stalls, the structure was completely rebuilt in the 1950s and now handles half a million customers daily. Don't let the swarms of shoppers deter from your enjoyment of the ornate interior, resplendent with walking bridges, fountains, and a glass-paneled roof. Anyone who might have visited GUM before the nineties will be shocked to see such European outlets as Galeries Lafayette, Benetton, and Escada occupying spaces priorly containing rows of barren state-owned stalls.

The **State Historical Museum** faces St. Basil's Cathedral from across the square. The multi-spired building was constructed in the late 1800s on the sight of the original Moscow University, founded in 1755. Containing an exhaustive exhibit of historical artifacts ranging from manuscripts, books, and coins to Peter the Great's sled and Napoleon's saber, the exhibition attempts and fairly well succeeds at documenting the hypocrisy that is Russian history since the Stone Ages.

The Arbat (Arbat Street)

The Arbat is a stop on the Moscow shore excursion itinerary because it offers the type of environment that tourists love— a cobblestone pedestrian thoroughfare full of shops and cafés that, in spite of its crowds, somehow seems more manageable to Westerners than most other parts of Moscow. But the Arbat is also a historic heart, a onetime entrance into the Muscovy capital, a 16th century home to courtiers, and 19th century neighborhood of aristocrats, artists, and writers.

The Arbat formerly encompassed an area that is now divided into the New Arbat (*Noviy Arbat*) and the old Arbat (simply *Arbat*). The quaint shopping zone, or Arbat Street itself, constitutes the old Arbat, on which tours concentrate. New Arbat refers to the strip of Prospekt Kalinina that parallels Arbat Street and was laid by bulldozing the Arbat's original main square, a monastery, and half a dozen churches. New Arbat is hence just another wide and noisy Moscow avenue. Arbat Street, which stretches from the yellow building containing the Praga restaurant to the "Stalinist Gothic" skyscraper housing the Foreign Ministry, lies mercifully insulated from the rat race—although its pocket-picking bands of gypsies and aggressive street vendors do present some sense of menace.

Considered by disparaging sorts a mere tourist trap, Arbat Street is definitely worth strolling, as it is probably the easiest place in the city to snack, shop, and people-watch. Certainly it buzzes with foreign dialects, but it remains a popular meeting spot for locals as well. Allow your attention from time to time to drift away from the lively street artists and performers in order to take in the colorful facades of old merchant shops. Collectors can find rare books and antiques along Arbat Street; the homesick can find relief at MacDonalds or Baskin-Robbins.

THE INSIDE SCOOP

There obviously is quite a bit to be scooped in this sprawling capital city. Again, using a Moscow-dedicated guidebook can be helpful if the ship's program isn't to your liking or if you're spending a few extra days here. Local publications that can shed some light on current happenings and hot-spots include two English language newspapers, *Moscow Times* and *Moscow Tribune*, as well as English language periodicals, *Moscow Magazine* and *Moscow Guardian*.

Moscow shore excursions are a mixed bag and are briefly reviewed below. Because of the distance between the Northern River Terminal and the downtown area, all tours utilize buses. Some people will be more than satisfied to go on all guided excursions, some will want to pick and choose, and others might elect to avoid them altogether. Whenever you do strike out on your own, don't forget that the tour buses can offer free and easy transportation into town. Also bear in mind that groups sometimes are shuttled back to the ship for lunch, a process that consumes as much as two to three hours and might warrant skipping.

Organized Shore Excursions

An excursion always offered by ships is called simply the "City Tour." It is a good outing for anyone who wants to get a general overview of Moscow and doesn't mind doing so from the inside of a chartered bus. You are let off the bus occasionally to serve as bait for souvenir-hawkers. You will pass every point of interest in the city; your task is to try to maintain your bearings. In general, a very touristy thing to do, but a very useful one as well.

The "Kremlin Tour" is the one excursion not to be missed. Individual admission to the Kremlin oftentimes can be restricted and/or difficult; therefore you possess a distinct advantage being with a sanctioned group. Moreover, this outing usually includes a visit to the spectacular Armory Chamber. It's a whirlwind tour of the exhibition, but it's the only one you'll get that's devoid of major admission hassles.

A visit to Red Square is sometimes included in the City Tour, sometimes in the Kremlin Tour, and sometimes added to another excursion. Because of its central location, Red Square can easily be made part of your own personal outing, which might include shopping at GUM or a swanky dinner at the Metropol. The outdoor patio of the Smirnoff Bar, accessible through a shoe store on the first floor of GUM, is also tempting, as it is the only place where you can repose right on Red Square while enjoying a cappuccino or draught beer. Yes, you pay heftily for the privilege

A "Metro Tour" is sometimes conducted. Your guide will simply herd your group underground to travel on the subway. It sounds a bit strange, but the Moscow Metro is unique in that its stations are clean and elaborately decorated with socialist artwork, ranging from mosaics to sculptures to stained glass (and lately, a few electric Marlboro signs). The physical depth of the stations, the lightning fast escalators, and the unbelievable size of the aggressive crowds add to the spectacle. If you're not the type to use the metro on your own during your stay, you owe it to yourself to tour it. Hardier types who will travel by metro at least a few times on their own should probably forego the group tour.

The "Arbat Street Tour" isn't really a tour at all, but rather a bus ride to Arbat Street where you are set free for a shopping spree. Of course there is much more to Arbat Street than shopping (you can stuff your face with pizza and ice cream), which makes it a worthy destination. However, if you don't relish the idea of making an en masse tourist *entrée*, or if you want to linger in the Arbat longer than the allotted time (perhaps for a meal), then you might pass on one or both bus rides.

Some ships offer a "Sergiev Posad (Zagorsk) Tour." This excursion entails a day trip by bus to the environs of Moscow for a visit to Russia's most famous Golden Ring destination, the Trinity Monastery of St. Sergius in the town of Sergiev Posad, formerly called Zagorsk. Advice on this one is tough. On one hand, you certainly see more than enough monasteries during the river voyage. On the other hand, the Trinity Monastery is the mother of all Russian monasteries. The monastery itself is absolutely breathtaking, the surroundings, including a lovely park, are serene and offer the potential for a lakeside picnic, and the two-hour, one-way bus ride provides a chance to survey the outer-Moscow landscape. Then again, four hours on a bus are four hours on a bus.

Most ships offer evening excursions to various cultural events, including the ballet, opera, etc. Some of the performances are truly first-rate; others are put together for large tourist groups and are truly bogus. Productions at the Kremlin State Palace are usually of the latter variety. You'll have to go on your own knowledge to determine what sounds good and what doesn't. At least make sure the musical accompaniment for a given performance is provided by a live orchestra. Unfortunately the Bolshoy Theater's first-string dance company tours the globe during summers. They're probably pirouetting in your home town right now.

Other Possibilities

Popular sights that are easily accessible and often neglected by shore excursions include the following:

Pushkin State Fine Arts Museum (Kropotkinskaya metro): Probably the most enjoyable fine art museum in all of Russia. Sure, the Hermitage in St. Petersburg is bigger, but what can you look at there besides the backs of peoples' heads? This spacious yet manageable museum boasts a discerning collection of European painting, an impressive exhibition of Egyptian art, and a smattering of really bad copies of Greek sculptures. It also frequently hosts world-renowned traveling exhibitions.

Gorky Park (Park Kultury metro): Occasionally tour groups from the ship attend the tented circus located in Gorky Park. They usually are not given the time to walk around the park itself, however, which is a pity. Spending an afternoon in renowned Gorky Park is certainly worthwhile, as it provides opportunity to glimpse Russian-style recreation. With scenic lakes, bridges, gardens, a fun zone, outdoor cafés serving *shashlik* and beer, and now even bungee jumping, there's something here for everyone.

Izmailovsky Park (Izmailovsky Park metro): The biggest weekend flea market in Moscow. All of your souvenir needs—from kitsch to valuable lacquer boxes to Soviet cameras to icons—can be met here in one mad shopping spree. Bargain hard, take a big bag, be Zen.

Kuznetsky Most (Kuznetsky Most metro): Formerly aristocratic shopping grounds, this centrally located neighborhood makes for colorful wanderings, with tasty street food, fashionable clothing shops, an English bookstore, and an excellent Georgian restaurant called Iberia. The Savoy Hotel, with four-star amenities, is nearby for a fix of Western elegance.

Okhotniy Ryad (metro Okhotniy Ryad): Moscow's first Western-style shopping mall, opened in 1998. Actually swankier than most in the West, this underground complex with lovely strolling grounds overhead will satisfy the most discerning mallaholic, but who on earth can afford to shop here?.

Past Dusk

Why spend evenings on the ship while docked in Moscow? The ship's bar follows you during the entire cruise, so forget about it for now and get yourself downtown. A few ships have been known to offer small sightseeing excursions at night. These are recommended, as Moscow by night presents an altogether different picture than by day.

Everybody must see Red Square at night. Whether you get there by guided tour, taxi, or metro, the floodlit Red Square with St. Basil's Cathedral looming as if from an alien fairy tale is an unforgettable travel memory.

Although it may not resemble San Francisco's North Beach in terms of visible nightlife, Moscow abounds with cabarets, casinos, restaurants, and clubs. Everything is just a bit hidden and dispersed. Before rushing off to a hyped variety show, bear in mind that Moscow is rated the most expensive city in the world outside of Japan. The place can really drain your wallet because inexpensive local joints are impossible to find and what is easily accessible is always pricy. Whatever you do, stay away from a cabaret show called Russkaya Troika.

Probably the best way to minimize the damage is to stick to a restaurant. Every kind of cuisine is available in Moscow and will cost you only slightly more than it does at home. For a few bucks the concierge at the Metropol will produce his detailed list of Moscow restaurants and even make reservations for you. Restaurant Praga at the top of Arbat Street offers a chance to sample traditional Russian *haute cuisine*; the cold plates alone, consisting of vegetables, caviar, salmon, cheese, etc., are a meal in themselves. For those who don't care to sample traditional Russian cuisine anymore, head to Azteca, a quaint Mexican restaurant located in a remodeled top-floor hotel room in the Intourist Hotel on Tverskaya Ulitsa. The food is surprisingly authentic and the panoramic view of Moscow is stupendous. And for those homesick Americans, Moscow now even offers TGI Friday's, one outside the Tverskaya metro station and one in the Okhotniy Ryad Mall.

UGLICH

ORIENTATION
A 1916 Volga guidebook remarks, "The city of Uglich is not in the present, it all lives in the past." Unfortunately not much has changed here since 1916, which means that Uglich, historically located on the right bank of the Volga but now on the bank of a reservoir, features a renowned ancient kremlin in a very provincial setting.

HISTORY
In 937 an envoy of Kievan Prince Igor visited a Slavonic trading settlement on the high right bank of the Volga to "register the population." In other words, Prince Igor decided it was time to familiarize the Slavs with the concept of taxation, and he sent a representative to make the arrangement legitimate by "founding" a town. The Slavs were not amused and eventually got around to tying Prince Igor between two bent trees and letting them—and him—rip. So goes the embellished legend of the origin of Uglich.

The town's officially recognized founding, however, is in 1148, the date it was first mentioned in the Chronicles. The town's name is explained by three separate theories: The first is that it is derived from the Russian word *ugol*, meaning "angle," for the Volga makes a sharp bend at Uglich; the second is that it is again derived from the Russian word *ugol*, which also means "coal," for coal was burned here; the third is that it is derived from the name of the town's original settlers, a Finno-Ugric tribe supposedly called *Uglichy*.

Established as its own principality in 1218, yet controlled by the Rostov-Suzdal principality throughout the 13th century, the popular Volga port thrived despite being sacked a couple of times by the pesky Mongol-Tatars. In 1326 Moscow Grand Prince Ivan (the Moneybags) purchased the flourishing principality for Muscovy. Under the

6.

7.

8.

9.

10.

local rule of Prince Andrey (the Big), Uglich reached the peak of its prosperity in the mid-15th century. The city's kremlin was fortified with formidable wooden walls which enclosed a palace complex, monastery, cathedral, and trading bazaar. The small principality even minted its own currency. A fire in 1491 devoured most of the wooden kremlin.

In 1552 Uglich bustled with activity as carpenters in the local forest assembled a portable wooden fortress for Ivan the Terrible to take with him to Kazan and use in his successful battle against the Tatars.

In 1591 perhaps the most famous event in Uglich's history occurred: the death of Ivan the Terrible's only living heir, Dmitry. It was widely believed that Boris Godunov orchestrated Dmitry's murder. Uglich townspeople got in big trouble for killing several of Godunov's henchmen when a tribunal ruled that the tsarevich's death actually was due to his having an epileptic seizure while playing with a knife. Whatever really happened, Dmitry's death sparked a subsequent power struggle for the throne, initially won by Godunov. Godunov's own death in 1605 then sparked the virtual craziness that was the Time of Troubles. The "False Dmitrys" mentioned so often in connection with the Time of Troubles were actually pretenders to the throne alleging to be grown-up Tsarevich Dmitry, miraculously not murdered here after all.

Foreign armies, most prominently the Polish, took advantage of the political instability and began driving toward Moscow. Somewhat of a bulwark for the capital, Uglich fell under repeated attack by the Poles, starting in 1608. In 1611 the city was obliterated and the population practically eradicated in one final gory confrontation with Swedes, who were also preparing to lay siege to Moscow.

Resilient as ever, Uglich gradually recovered. By the end of the 17th century it had become a destination of religious pilgrimage due to the founding of the Church of St. Dmitry on the Blood, built to honor the slain tsarevich, who had since been canonized. New kremlin walls, this time of stone, were built along with the church. The Transfiguration Cathedral was added to the complex in 1713, one year before Peter the Great forbid stone buildings anywhere but in St. Petersburg. Peter's decrees, nonetheless, took their toll on Uglich's development. All the city's bells were melted to make artillery for the Northern War with Sweden, and the male population was summoned to St. Petersburg to either enlist in the navy or help construct showy stone buildings.

Some fifty years after Peter's reign Russia's second most fervent Westernizer, Catherine the Great, visited Uglich. The empress was greatly impressed, although she ordered the town's layout changed in accordance with her general reconstruction plan for all Russian towns to become more symmetrical (i.e., more European). Uglich complied with the imperial request, adding Neo-Classical civic structures, stone churches, and stone dwellings to its newly straightened streets. (Peter's prohibition on stone structures had been lifted by this time.)

The 19th century issued in the decline of Uglich. Additions to the Mariinskaya Canal System altered the dynamics of river travel such that ships stopped at Rybinsk, to the northeast, rather than at Uglich. Not connected to vital centers by railway, Uglich saw one half of its enterprises fail and a large portion of its population migrate to more active areas. Yet the city of uncommon beauty and rich history began to lure artists, writers, and historians who fueled a revival of Uglich's heritage. In spite of economic decline, cultural institutions were established, among them a new local studies museum and library. Mikhail Chekhov, brother of the famous writer, took up residence in the town, founding a theatrical society. In addition to working as a theater critic and journalist, Chekhov also brought a degree of historical closure to Uglich by functioning as a tax assessor.

Four years prior to the 1917 Revolution, a city guide-book remarked, "Uglich is a sleepy town on the Volga River. Its glory is over, and it is difficult to believe that life will start here again." The Soviet government, however, saw to it that activity resumed in Uglich—which is not to say that Uglich was enlivened or enhanced. Stalin's second and third Five-Year Plans (1935-40) called for the implementation of a hydroplant at Uglich as part of the overall plan to harness the Volga for hydroelectricity. Uglich suddenly became the base for a large-scale engineering undertaking. The city also gained a stone-cutting plant and cheese manu-factory.

The reality of Uglich's 20th century revival, though, is best described by a post-*glasnost* city guidebook. With resigned understatement it remarks:

> Unfortunately, the town also lost a great deal.
> Half of its churches were demolished, monas-
> tery walls were taken down, which detracted
> greatly from the appearance of the ensemble,
> and the old Monastery of the Intercession, with
> some unique monuments of the 15th, 16th,
> and 17th centuries, was blown up and flooded.
> At one time it was the most distinguishing
> feature of the southwest outskirts of the town.
> The huge building of the hydropower station
> was erected in its place.

In 1952, with Stalin mercifully one year away from death, a so-called restoration unit was set up in Uglich to save the town's monuments from further destruction and neglect. This was Soviet bureaucracy at its best, for the unit, well, did nothing. It sat by and watched while several unsightly five-story modern constructions were placed in the middle of the town center and thoughtless alterations were made to many historic structures especially in the 1960s. Recently a new general plan for the development of Uglich was adopted, calling for conservation zones and building regulations. Whether the new plan's impact will be felt remains to be seen.

ABOUT THE CITY

Unlike the traveling peasantry of Kostroma, the Uglich citizenry is historically characterized by a love for domesticity and familiarity. The town's 19th century decline was attributed by some observers to the populace's tradition of trading amongst themselves without much interest in the outside world and without much profit. Domestic people are dedicated and driven though, and indeed Uglichers have continued to maintain the various industries established here in the early century. Aside from machine-building and jobs related to the operation of the Uglich Hydroplant, the city is involved in cheese-making and watch-manufacturing. The Chaika watch factory hammers out five million timepieces a year in a plant at the edge of town. The distinct, enamel-banded watches are available in a few downtown shops and embankment kiosks. Famous Uglich cheese is also processed on the outskirts of town; but honestly speaking, we can't figure out why it's famous.

Denizens of Uglich are also known to take advantage of the surrounding countryside, still endowed with coniferous forests in spite of industrial exploitation. An excerpt from a recent local guidebook paints a more vivid picture with characteristic wryness: "In spite of the intensive felling and the high voltage cables and gas pipelines running across them, the Uglich forests still give hours of pleasure to mushroom-pickers, hunters, and hikers."

SIGHTS

Shore excursions in Uglich tend to concentrate solely on Uglich's old kremlin with its riverfront aspect and ancient buildings. The fortress itself long ago lost its formidable appearance. Only traces of its stone walls can be seen, as well as sections of the original moat, which after 15th century expansion, was actually located inside the fortress and therefore mostly filled in. The northwest section of the moat survives, however, functioning today as a colorful harbor for small boats.

Entering the kremlin and crossing the old moat, you approach the **Transfiguration Cathedral**, perched at the water's edge. Built in 1713, the green-domed cathedral is an active place of Orthodox worship, often resounding with religious singing. Even without ethereal background music the interior is awesome. The high vaulted ceiling unsupported by pillars not only creates a much lighter sense of drama than in a Gothic cathedral, but represents quite an engineering feat for its day. The splendid Baroque iconostasis adds to the inspirational effect. Set off from the nave is an exhibition of valuable icons and religious artifacts through which local guides usually conduct a fairly educational tour.

Outside, the cathedral's elegant belfry stands thirty-seven meters high, crowned by a gilded dome recognizable from great distances. The Chaika watch factory installed an electronic bell in the tower in 1984; its ringing can be heard every half hour. You are not allowed to climb the bell tower, but you should go into the small antique shop located within.

The red **Church of St. Dmitry on the Blood**, perhaps the most fascinating edifice in the kremlin, stands nearby. Built in 1692 after the canonization of murdered Tsarevich Dmitry, the structure is a fine example of 17th century church architecture, designed with a love of embellishment, rich ornamentation, and striking colors. Somewhat resembling a red and blue birthday cake due to its ornate windows, decorative cornice, series of pilasters, and star-studded cupolas, the church cannot help but enchant. The effect may not be entirely appropriate, considering the rather grisly event the building memorializes. However, the size of the structure is relatively modest, making for an intimate interior. Frescoes cover virtually all inner components, adding a dazzling presentation of color to the tight proportions. In the narthex-refectory, the portrayal of an unclothed Adam and Eve is an anomaly for Orthodox Church wall paintings. (Because the church was intended more as a commemorative structure than as a functional one, the powers-that-be evidently allowed the painters to take some liberties with Orthodox traditions.) On the walls of the tiny nave the legend of the murder of Dmitry is painted in an intriguing narrative style. The exiled bell of Uglich is here also. When Boris Godunov and his cronies were cleared of the murder of Dmitry, the ruling tribunal not only punished the townspeople of Uglich for having exacted retribution on the alleged assailants, but it also sentenced the bell that had rung out to alert the town of the crime. The bell was lashed, deprived of its tongue and one ear, and exiled to Siberia. It seems happier now that it's back home. In front of the iconostasis lies the final element in the story of the murdered tsarevich: the litter on which the boy's exhumed corpse was carried to Moscow to prove that Dmitry was indeed deceased, thus precluding the appearance of any more False Dmitrys.

Another stop on the kremlin tour, the **Palace Chamber**, is a surviving section of the original palace complex built by Prince Andrey the Big in the 15th century. Altered and added to several times since its founding, the structure is a peculiar hybrid of original medieval architecture and curious subsequent additions. It is, however, one of the oldest civic structures standing in this part of Russia. It now houses a museum of local antiquities, containing ho-hum displays of fabrics, tiles, and other applied arts.

THE INSIDE SCOOP

The walking tour of the kremlin—the main activity of the stop—is worthwhile. You might want to beat the groups there, though, to have at least a few minutes to experience the sublime ambiance of the churches before taking part in the tourist invasion. By the way, groups will usually shy away from the green-domed Transfiguration Cathedral if an Orthodox service is being held inside. You, however, are welcome to observe the mesmerizing ritual on your own (provided you cover your head if you are a woman). If the cathedral is inactive on the day of your visit, never fear— ambiance is often provided by a quartet of Orthodox singers which performs a few somber chants for visiting groups. The only difference between the quartet and the authentic choir is that the former has a tip-box and peddles cassettes.

The antique shop in the cathedral's belfry actually is not a bad place to pick up genuine artifacts like silver, jewelry, tsarist rubles, etc. If you purchase an authentic icon, beware that you will have to smuggle it out of the country—no matter what the salesman says.

Chaika watches are always a tourist obsession in Uglich—rightly so, as they fetch up to $200 in the States while here you can pick one up for one-tenth that price. Try the souvenir shop downtown and the kiosks in the park along the quay. If all else fails, you can try walking out to the factory store, in the opposite direction from the city along the quay. The locals hawking watches along the promenade may or may not have genuine Chaikas, but they offer good prices if you haggle a bit. To disclose a secret, the only difference in Uglich between "fake" and real Chaikas is that the former are assembled by private individuals using parts stolen from the factory—and they're reportedly much more reliable.

Uglich, surprisingly, is not a bad place at all to buy Russian souvenirs. At last check, there was only one major downtown souvenir shop, and you will of course be herded into it by local guides. The makeshift farmers' market outside the shop seems to grow every year, as does the size of the suspect fresh vegetables (but the mushrooms and berries truly are divine). On the side streets, state shops that used to sell things like bread and shoes are increasingly becoming private shops peddling staples like premium liquor and imported confectionery.

For some reason, ships tend to spend very little time docked at Uglich. Usually you have just enough time to tour the kremlin, buy a few souvenirs, and get back on board before departure. If, however, you have a longer stay here (or if you've visited the kremlin before), you might journey out to some of Uglich's other famous religious ensembles such as the 18th century Resurrection Monastery, the Epiphany Convent, or the Monastery of St. Alexiy.

Or, for a little fun and recreation, you might hire a paddleboat and cruise around out on the Uglich Reservoir. The rental boatyard is located right off the embankment promenade on your way to town. All you need is your passport for a deposit and about a dollar for an hour's rental. Take your camera—this is an opportunity to photograph the Uglich churches from an unbeatabl perspective!

YAROSLAVL

ORIENTATION
Yaroslavl is among the oldest and most well known of all Russian provincial cities. A prosperous mercantile center in the past, the city boasts a plethora of dazzling merchant churches and a lovely riverfront aspect.

HISTORY
From the 8th to 10th century, Finno-Ugric tribes occupied the towering banks above the Volga where the river is joined by a tributary, the Kotorosl River. The outpost was called Bear Corner, as the pagan Finno-Ugrics revered and worshipped bears. Occasionally the tribes would exploit their privileged riverfront position and ambush passing merchant ships. Entreated by aggravated merchants, Rostov Prince Yaroslavl the Wise, along with some trusty men-at-arms, sailed past the settlement and successfully defended the merchants. Pious Prince Yaroslavl then went ashore to talk the local inhabitants out of their errant pagan ways. The tribesmen responded by sicking a ferocious bear on him. In what must have been an impressive wrestling match, Prince Yaroslavl killed the bear, winning the submission of the amazed onlookers. He ordered a church built and founded the city; the tribes were in no mood to argue. Thus recounts the legend of the founding of ancient Yaroslavl in 1010.

In 1218 Yaroslavl became the capital of its own principality. This was the era of Mongol-Tatar invasions, and the city did not escape the invaders' wrath, being sacked and burned to the ground in 1238. However, it remained an independent principality and important port for the next 225 years. Ivan the Great annexed the principality to Muscovy in 1463 during his surge for unification of the Russian lands. At the onset of the Time of Troubles in 1598, the Russian capital was transferred temporarily to Yaroslavl from imperiled Moscow. In 1612, with Moscow occupied by the

Polish army, Russian heroes Minin and Pozharsky consolidated their citizens' army in Yaroslavl, going on to march on Moscow and evict the Poles. Skillful Cossack mercenaries lent a decisive hand during the battle, and the Time of Troubles was ended.

With order in the country restored and young Michael Romanov seated on the throne, the capital was moved back to Moscow in 1613. Yaroslavl suffered not. From 1613 to 1703 the city enjoyed a spectacular golden age, becoming the most prominent mercantile center of the upper Volga region. Trade routes from the Middle East and Europe converged on Yaroslavl, where merchants exchanged goods made of leather, silver, wood, and exotic fabrics. One-sixth of Russia's wealthiest merchant families kept homes in Yaroslavl at this time; their neighbors were often fellow traders from England or Holland.

The city's mercantile success spelled two things: churches and more churches. In order to stay in God's (and the Church's) good graces and also to one-up their more cosmopolitan southern neighbors in Moscow, wealthy merchant families sponsored the building of skillfully crafted and opulently adorned religious edifices. By the end of the 17th century, the city had erected no less than fifty new churches.

During the early 18th century Peter the Great saw to it that all attention focused on his new capital, St. Petersburg. Yaroslavl consequently fell from mercantile grace. The city persevered nevertheless, developing industry and encouraging cultural growth. Russia's first national theater was founded in Yaroslavl in 1750, and the country's first major provincial newspaper was established here in 1786.

Industry continued to rear its ugly head. By the middle of the 19th century, twelve textile plants and nearly seventy various factories were steadily ejecting their fumes into the Volga air. A railroad to Moscow was laid in 1870, fostering continued growth. As is often the case, unregulated industrial expansion also nurtured worker discontent. As Soviet history relates, "The workers [of Yaroslavl] earned a mere pittance, went cold and hungry, and worked from sixteen to eighteen hours a day. Capitalist exploitation and lack of political rights led them to rise up against their oppressors." Textile workers organized a strike in 1895. The 1917 Bolshevik Revolution was soon to follow.

After Yaroslavl was ruined by bloody post-revolution skirmishes between Red and White Guards during the Civil War, the city settled obediently into its new Soviet role. The role constituted nothing new, just industrial expansion and technological development with a vengeance. During the 1930s Yaroslavl's factories turned out the Soviet Union's first heavy-duty trucks, its first trolley buses, and its first diesel engines. The local rubber plant boasted of mass-producing the world's first synthetic rubber tires.

Today Yaroslavl's colorful ancient history and its comparatively muted recent history compete to define the city. A recent Russian guidebook calls Yaroslavl "one of Russia's most polluted cities"; yet the effects of the damage done by mankind's advances are not nearly as visible as elsewhere along the Volga. A combination of the seventy year rule of the atheistic Soviets and the reckless progress spearheaded by some of its more notorious leaders resulted in the neglect and disappearance of many of Yaroslavl's famous churches; yet several of the city's most splendid structures survive.

ABOUT THE CITY
Connected to Moscow (as well as to the rest of the country) by all major transportation routes, including 280 kilometers of bandit-ridden highway, Yaroslavl remains an important commercial center. Most of the population of 650,000 work in the various local industries, including oil refining and manufacturing of rubber tires, diesel engines, textiles, enamels, and paints. Additionally, the city is a livestock farming center, raising the supposedly world-renowned

Romanovskaya sheep in addition to an allegedly distinctive breed of cattle. Perhaps having something to do with the distinctive cows, cheese from Yaroslavl is said to have been distinguished in international competitions. Whether or not you'll find any prize-winning *syr* in the shops is another story.

SIGHTS

Although local sightseeing tours all differ somewhat, brace yourself for a string of churches. The ones never missed are here briefly described.

A frequent warm-up stop for shore excursions is the red brick **Church of the Epiphany**, built in 1684-93. This striking building, whose green roofs and bluish-green cupolas complement the main body, is known for its 17th century handcrafted glazed tiles adorning the exterior. Local craftsmen have actually replaced some of the original, defiled tiles with reproductions, which means that experts on glazed, handcrafted, Volga-region ceramic work will have a field day trying to distinguish the new tiles from the old ones. Or, since no such experts likely exist, anybody can have some fun trying to differentiate the replacements from the authentics. Inside the church, frescoes painted in 1693 depict the life of Christ. The seven-tiered, gilded iconostasis rounds out the impressive interior.

The **Church of St. Elijah the Prophet** is a mainstay on the local tour itinerary and deservedly so. Built in 1647-50, the church features a unique, asymmetrical exterior (created by five unevenly arranged green cupolas on the main building), covered galleries, a belfry, portico, and bulky spire of an adjoining chapel. The compelling overall effect is surpassed only by that of the treasures inside the building. Frescoes painted in 1680 by renowned Kostroma artists blanket the entire interior. Nothing is left uncovered by the lively illustrative painting; the walls of the church as well as the galleries, vaults, piers, window sills and portals are all graced with artisans' original pigments. An especially impressed visitor once remarked on the overall effect: "It seems to flow like a solemn, festive ode to the joy of living." The church's lace-like iconostasis, undertaken in 1696, is regarded as a masterpiece of Russian Baroque. Its icons date primarily from the 1670s. The 1660 carved wooden thrones for the tsar and patriarch are also superb examples of the crafts of antiquity. The list goes on and on... Your local guide will certainly fill you in on the rest.

If the paved expanse (Ilyinskaya Square) engulfing the St. Elijah Church seems a bit too expansive, it is because Catherine the Great was so impressed with the church that she ordered all surrounding dwellings cleared away to maximize the structure's visibility. You can bet the Skripkin merchant family, whose home was ordered moved, were a bit miffed, as they paid for the church's construction. Also, while standing in the square take note of the Soviet Executive Committee building (you'll know which one it is). It was designed to blend in with the square's earlier structures. Does it succeed?

The main sightseeing destination in Yaroslavl is the **Savior-Transfiguration Monastery**. Founded in the 12th century, the monastery is one of the Volga's oldest and a regional sentimental favorite. Halfhearted restoration indicated by perpetually vacant scaffolding has been under way for as long as any local guide can remember. Yet most of what made the monastery one of the richest and best fortified in Russia survives. The gold-domed Transfiguration Cathedral, subsidiary chapels, main belfry, monks' cells, and three meter-thick fortress walls were all undertaken at various times during the 16th and 17th centuries. Try to imagine the scene of soldiers atop the fortress walls pouring boiling oil on their attackers in the midst of battle— it really happened here. In fact, the army that liberated Moscow during the Time of Troubles was assembled in

Yaroslavl precisely because foreign invaders could not penetrate the monastery.

An area of the city not mentioned during shore excursions beyond a few introductory words is Yaroslavl's **embankment**, one of the most pleasant to be found among all Volga towns. The embankment, landscaped in the mid-19th century, comprises a long promenade bordered by a picturesque greenbelt referred to as "linden tree alley." The colonnaded gazebos, perched atop the bank, afford wonderful Volga panoramas. Should you opt to stroll leisurely along the promenade instead of exploring historical monuments, beware—two historic churches stand on the quay. At Number Five stands the St. Elijah and St. Tikhon Church, built in 1830. Regarded as a masterpiece of "Russian Classicism," the structure is in disrepair and may or may not be open to visitors. However, hidden in the nearby courtyard at Number Two, the 1649 St. Nicholas Nadeina Church is usually tended by a *babushka* who charges a nominal entrance fee. The interior frescoes are in bad shape, yet the overall setting somehow produces an alluring atmosphere.

THE INSIDE SCOOP
Yaroslavl has more remarkable medieval wall paintings than any other Russian town, so you owe it to yourself to go on the bus tour and check them out. Some of the local guides here are excellent, as well. Some tips on how to maximize your experience of the tour itself include the following:

– At the Church of the Epiphany: Make sure to venture inside the church, as the interior is stunning. Oftentimes local guides don't want to spend more than five minutes here, beckoning tourists off the bus to photograph the church's exterior and then leaving.

– At the Church of St. Elijah the Prophet: It is interesting to observe the church from various distances in the surrounding square until you discover the privileged vantage point at which the asymmetry of the building's design slips into perfect symmetry.

– At the Savior-Transfiguration Monastery: First of all, at the entrance buy yourself a ticket that allows you to access the belfry. Groups don't climb the belfry for logistical reasons, but the view from the top is absolutely breathtaking. All this requires is a few extra dollars, a few extra minutes, and an indifference to heights. Second of all, you might want to take along a small snack for Masha, a huge brown bear who lives in a cage in the monastery. When Masha was a cub in the forest her mother was killed, and local children brought her to the monastery, where she's been staying ever since. The poor thing never learned to hunt—in fact she's a vegetarian!—so you may as well feed her a nutritious tidbit and snap a photograph.

Bus tours also usually stop somewhere near Yaroslavl's central bazaar, featuring 18th century arcades, to allow for shopping. This is not a bad place to pick up supplies such as local beer, vodka, small cakes, odd clothing items, toiletries, etc. There are a few typical cafés around here, too. All you need is a little time and the will to walk around for a while. If this is the last stop of the tour, don't be afraid to let the bus go back to the river terminal without you. It is an easy, ten-minute walk away. If you get lost, do what a Russian would do: stop the first passerby you see and ask *Gdye Volga*? (Where's the Volga?).

Recently some buses have been making a stop at the Yaroslavl Puppet Theater to listen to a fairly interesting talk by the theater director, take a look at the mildly interesting puppet exhibit in the lobby, and naturally, shop for souvenirs which are peddled wishfully by folks who are likely friends of your tour guide.

If shopping isn't your bag, and the tour hasn't inclined you to agree with the opinion of Russian poet Apolon Grigoriev who wrote, "The beauty of Yaroslavl cannot be described. Everywhere there is Volga, everywhere there is history," then it might be time for you to take a stroll along the embankment promenade to relax. The two churches along the quay provide an opportunity to visit places of historical, religious, and artistic significance unhindered by the occasional pitfalls of tour group dynamics. You might also visit the two quaint private museums located along the embankment: the enchanting Museum of Time and Music, which is the former home of a German composer who dabbled in watchmaking (or vice-versa), and the adjacent Museum of One Picture, whose name alone should suffice to draw you inside. Admission to each costs approximately one dollar.

For those who can stand the boat restaurant no longer, an excellent Hungarian restaurant called Hungaria can be reached in twenty minutes walk or better yet, by taxi. A little closer to "home" is a Georgian restaurant located in the river terminal right beneath the lookout tower. With terrific food and wine, the place also boasts a very lively ambiance in the evenings. For those looking to add that chic touch to their visit, try to make reservations for dinner in the city's most exclusive restaurant located in a tower of the Transfiguration Monastery. Take lots of rubles for these establishments; credit cards, at last check, were still looked at with curiosity.

KOSTROMA

ORIENTATION

Situated farther down the Volga than Yaroslavl, the town of Kostroma actually is located 128 kilometers to the northeast of Yaroslavl, as the two historic settlements sit at opposite ends of a Volga digression. Regarded as preserving the feel of typical Russian provinces, Kostroma is often used as the setting for films and literature. Kostroma is also famous for its Ipatievsky Monastery, where the first tsar of the Romanov dynasty accepted the throne.

HISTORY

First mentioned in the Chronicles in 1237, Kostroma was founded somewhat earlier than that by pagan Slavs. *Kostroma* (pronounced with the last syllable stressed) was the name of a pagan god. On their way to sacking Yaroslavl in 1238, invading Mongol-Tatars first stopped in Kostroma for a dress rehearsal. Nonetheless by the mid-13th century the town had recovered and was an important port of the Vladimir principality.

In the 17th century the chaos of the Time of Troubles officially ended when young Michael Romanov accepted the Russian throne from his place of hiding in Kostroma's Ipatievsky Monastery. With order reestablished, Kostroma flourished alongside Yaroslavl, becoming the country's third most important city (behind Moscow and Yaroslavl). During this period the city prospered on trade with the Middle East and boasted some of the country's finest fresco painters, who often were summoned to Yaroslavl to beautify the many churches being built there.

Kostroma's significance began to dwindle upon the founding of Russia's new capital, St. Petersburg. The town turned from mercantilism to manufacturing, although never entirely surrendering its role as an important Volga port. In 1773 a major fire devoured most of Kostroma. The city center was built anew, and by the end of the 18th century Kostroma had not only recovered, but established itself as a growing manufacturer of flax. By the turn of the century the city was known as the "flax capital," supplying Russia and Europe with the very finest cloth with which to fabricate sails.

The city's glory days were long gone by the beginning of the 20th century. Kostroma plodded along suffering many of the same woes as its Volga neighbors: unregulated industrial expansion, economic polarization, political oppression, etc. A 1903 visitor satirically described the city thus:

> The abundance of greenery, welcoming houses,
> and broad streets would have created a rather
> attractive appearance, were it not for the dust
> of the dry season and the mud of the rainy
> season. The sanitary state of the town cannot
> be envied, and the climate of Kostroma isn't
> quite healthy. There is nearly no movement in
> the streets and only during the navigation and
> on days of church processions (which occur
> about 100 times a year) does the town show
> signs of life.

The bulk of Kostroma's 20th century history reads more or less like that of Yaroslavl: declaration of Soviet power, Civil War, nationalization of industrial and agricultural enterprises, razing of churches, economic stagnation, etc.

ABOUT THE CITY

Russian sources describe the Kostroma region as historically possessing a "peculiar peasantry." The men were known to be tall, handsome, worldly, good-spirited, intelligent, and enterprising—largely because they often traveled to distant regions to peddle their wares. Incidentally, due to the frequent absence of men, the women were considered quite resourceful in their own right. Of course this entire characterization is derived from a quasi-evolutionary model, and evidence of it may not be readily apprehended by the passing visitor (or by anyone else, for that matter). Nonetheless it provides an amusing perspective from which to view Kostroma's modern-day citizenry.

The present population of 300,000 is engaged in a variety of enterprises, including Kostroma's historically famed endeavor of producing flax, sixty percent of which is exported abroad. Excavators, automobile engines, and plywood are also produced here. Like other historic Volga towns, Kostroma is a popular tourist destination, hosting 650,000 visitors annually.

SIGHTS

A staple on the Kostroma tour is a stop in the 18th century, fanlike **city center**. For some reason local guides and guidebooks are extremely fond of pointing out that Kostroma is one of the only Russian towns to preserve its "original city center layout." It's a dubious statement, for the city center was conceived by a pair of St. Petersburg architects put in charge of *redesigning* it after a great fire destroyed the original one in 1773. With or without a fire, the city plan likely would have been overhauled anyway, as during the rule of Catherine the Great (1762-96), the empress ordered more than one hundred provincial towns to straighten their streets and become more symmetrical, like European cities. Original or not, there is no disputing the peculiar charm of the center, boasting more trading arcades than almost any other Russian town. Formerly each arcade had a separate designation (flour arcade, fish arcade, butter arcade, etc.). Today a small open-air market still is held downtown; many arcades, however, are either vacant or occupied by something a little strange, like an electronics shop or an ice cream parlor. Around the hub of the town center (the main square) stand a 19th century firehouse tower, an 18th century hotel, a courthouse (once a 19th century palace), a registry (once a jail), and town hall. All main streets converge on the square, which sounds like an organized layout, but for some reason it's hard to keep your bearings while walking around Kostroma.

Across the Kostroma River, approximately six kilometers from the city center, stand the formidable bleach-white walls of the **Ipatievsky Monastery** with the glittering golden cupolas of its main cathedral hovering in the background. The monastery is the main attraction in Kostroma. Well-preserved and containing a variety of compelling exhibitions, the Ipatievsky is probably the most enthralling monastery of the cruise.

A Tatar prince named Chet, who was a Godunov ancestor, converted to Christianity and founded the Ipatievsky Monastery in 1332. The Godunovs subsequently adopted the monastery as their personal holy place, donating large sums of money for its continued growth and improvement. During Boris Godunov's reign (1598-1605), the monastery unsurprisingly became the country's wealthiest.

Boris's death in 1605 by no means spelled the end of the monastery's prosperity. On the contrary, it set in motion a chain of events which ultimately resulted in the monastery becoming one of the most significant in Russian history. During the internal strife and foreign intervention (the Time of Troubles) sparked by Boris Godunov's death, a young boyar named Michael Romanov, who was distantly related to Boris, took refuge in the monastery along with his mother, Sister Marfa. Once the Poles were cleared out of Moscow, an Assembly of the Land, consisting of Cossacks, Church officials, and military leaders, chose Michael to be the next tsar.

The Poles got wind of the decision and, not content to abandon their mission, went on a manhunt for the young boyar. Enter Ivan Susanin, a simple *muzhik* (peasant) turned folk hero. According to legend, Susanin met the Poles in his village of Domnino and offered to take them to the hiding place of the young tsar-in-waiting. He proceeded to lead the troops on a wild goose chase which eventually terminated in a swamp, after having sent a brother-in-law to warn the Ipatievsky Monastery of the threat. Once the Poles realized they had been bamboozled, they promptly made alligator meat out of Susanin. But their plans were foiled. The monastery had been sufficiently fortified and the conspirators whereabouts were revealed. The day—and the tsar— was saved.

At first, the *muzhik's* heroism seemed in vain, for Tsar-elect Michael steadfastly refused to accept the throne, probably fearing the daunting scope and omnipresent perils of the job. But on 4 March 1613 the Ipatievsky Monastery stood surrounded by the entire population of Kostroma anticipating his acceptance. Inside the compound were boyars, military commanders, Moscow ambassadors, bishops, the Holy Patriarch of Russia, and anyone else of high political station, all there to hail the ascension of the new tsar. Yet the young man of seventeen, abetted by his mother, remained unswayed by the grandiose speeches and heartfelt implorements, purportedly whimpering with internal strife throughout. Eventually so many people got on their knees that Michael consented. The church bells tolled and the crowd commenced singing. A new dynasty was born.

The Romanov family remained indebted to the monastery, bolstering its wealth throughout their reign. By the end of the 17th century the monastery owned 22,000 hectares of land and 17,000 serfs. It was also a regional cultural center, housing a library of rare books and manuscripts. When an explosion in 1649 destroyed the monastery's Trinity Cathedral, built in stone by the Godunovs in 1590 to replace the original 14th century wooden church, the Romanovs promptly had it rebuilt. The rather austere, gold-domed structure made of white stone is still the focal point of the monastery. Inside the cathedral 17th century frescoes rendered by renowned Kostroma painters cover the walls. The graves of most of the Godunov family are housed here also.

The Soviets turned the Ipatievsky Monastery into the Kostroma Museum of History and Architecture, a comparatively sterile designation, but one that at least enabled the monastery's preservation. By the time you get there, though, it may have been given back to the Orthodox Church. Regardless of what it's called or who holds the ownership papers, the compound contains several worthwhile exhibitions. In a block of monks' cells a small museum featuring icons and antique handicrafts generates more interest than most of its kind. The red brick Archbishop's House, across from the Trinity Cathedral, houses one of the most moving exhibitions to be found anywhere, the Romanov Family Exhibition, an intimate portrayal of the life and times of the last tsar, Nicholas II, and his family.

Finally, a favorite destination of many tourists is Kostroma's open-air **Museum of Wooden Architecture**, located in a serene setting adjacent to the monastery's fortress walls. Here amidst picturesque streams and woods stands a variety of handcrafted wooden structures from around the Kostroma region. Small churches, barns, windmills, boathouses, and a series of peasant dwellings ranging from the modest to the opulent are open for your inspection.

THE INSIDE SCOOP

Ground tours in Kostroma tend to be a little unpredictable. Sometimes local guides arrange a visit to a school or factory to appease those who have had their fill of monasteries. These visits are indeed rewarding for the slice of daily rural life they provide, yet the Ipatievsky Monastery *is* a real gem and probably shouldn't be missed. Furthermore, the Romanov Family Exhibition located within the monastery is a must for anyone interested in the tragic last chapter of Russia's flight from monarchy. A visit to this exhibition is not always included in the guided tour of the monastery, so you might have to buy admission tickets at the main entrance and break away from the group for a spell.

After touring the monastery, guides tend to herd their groups back into the bus to ride to the enjoyable open-air museum. This is sort of a ridiculous bus ride, as the museum grounds are located virtually right around the corner. Depending on time constraints, you might want to opt for a brief stroll to the museum. Reaching the monastery itself on foot from downtown, although plausible, is rather time-consuming and not particularly scenic. It's best to stick to the bus, or, in a pinch, to flag down a car.

While in Kostroma, keep your eyes out for *kvas* vendors. *Kvas* is a uniquely Russian, non-alcoholic beverage made from fermented black bread and served on the streets during summer months. Try a jar—it can really increase your sightseeing range on a hot day. The Cyrillic spelling for *kvas*, by the way, is "КВАС."

Like in Yaroslavl, the city center in Kostroma can offer interesting shopping possibilities. The farmers' market abounds with fruits and vegetables in summer. Antiques and other odd items can be found as well in the network of arcades. With a little time to meander through the arcades, you can discover cheap draught beer, expensive cheeses, even thousand dollar Italian home appliances. The city center is only a five minute walk from the river terminal, so don't feel at the mercy of the tour bus. Straying too far from the city center proper isn't exceptionally rewarding, unless you have a penchant for exploring rundown provincial neighborhoods.

Whatever you do, do not get suckered into a trip to Kostroma's flea market, located a few kilometers southeast of the city center. Local guides often suggest the flea market for shopping, but it is nothing more than a crowded swap meet full of useless odds and ends. You'll fare much better in the city center.

It's slim pickings in Kostroma for eating. A few typical cafés are hidden in the arcade on the main square, as well as along the main street. If you want to stock your cabin with little pizzas and *khachapury* (tasty Georgian cheese pies), head to café Uyoot (Russian for "coziness") in town square. They also serve traditional Russian coffee here, which tastes something like sweet mud. To get to the café, walk up the road leading away from the river terminal, past the park, until you reach the square. Turn left, and go past the first arcade. At the beginning of the next arcade, you'll see a little wooden sign near a slightly submerged door. It doesn't look cozy from the outside, but that's the place!

Alternatively, the newly opened Literaturnoye Café is a restaurant/bar/pizza parlor complex located in the opposite direction along the main street (Sovetskaya). Although the restaurant on the top floor is often closed, the pizza parlor in the basement offers a sparkling atmosphere, attentive service, and fairly respectable pizza and Italian dishes. And believe it or not, it is (gasp) a no-smoking establishment! Plus there is an outside "patio" area. To get to the Literaturnoye Café, make a right at the main square and walk along Sovetskaya to the first stoplight (Gornaya street). You'll see the café not far from the corner on the left side of the street.

NIZHNY NOVGOROD
– not visited by all ships –

ORIENTATION
Formerly called Gorky, this was the closed city to which the Soviet government exiled dissident physicist and social critic Andrey Sakharov in the 1980s. With its commanding views on the Volga and Oka rivers, its well-preserved ancient kremlin, respectable museums, and pleasant downtown, it's actually not a bad place to spend an exile, if one must. The historic city actually spreads on both sides of the Oka River, but the "new" (read: Soviet) part of town, lying on the side opposite the river terminal, holds zero interest for visitors. The old part of town, however, is a delight.

HISTORY
In order to consolidate the southeastern borders of the Vladimir-Suzdal principality, Prince Yury Vsevolodovich, one of many sons of Prince Vsevolod III (the Big Nest), ordered a fortress built on a high plateau in Woodpecker's Hills, which overlook the junction of the Volga and Oka rivers. Subjects from around the principality came to participate in the building of the earthen and wooden kremlin. Inhabitants of neighboring areas also migrated to the fortress's proximity for safety purposes and economic possibilities. The future "Volga capital" was born.

The year of groundbreaking was 1221, not a good time to found a city on the Volga, as Genghis Kahn and his ornery Mongol-Tatar army were on their way to Rus to lay waste to her principalities. Nonetheless the fortress sprung up rapidly. The city was named Nizhny Novgorod, which means "low new city," to distinguish it from other emerging Novgorods ("new cities"). Although the founding inhabitants managed to erect stone churches within their kremlin a full one hundred years before their Moscow' counterparts, they soon saw them razed to the ground, as Mongol-Tatars indeed sacked the place repeatedly from shortly after its founding up to the 15th century. Frequent fires and a 1364 outbreak of plague did not help the city get on its feet either.

By the 16th century the weakened Golden Horde could no longer topple the new stone kremlin. The Mongol-Tatars finally went home, leaving Nizhny Novgorod to flourish as a popular mercantile center and military outpost. When Muscovy (to which Nizhny Novgorod had been annexed in the 14th century) found itself again at the mercy of foreign invaders—this time the Poles occupying Moscow in 1610-13—Nizhny Novgorod's mayor, Kuzma Minin, along with a prince named Pozharsky, rallied an army and marched to the besieged capital. Picking up forces along the way and consolidating in Yaroslavl, the army liberated the capital. Minin became a national hero and Nizhny Novgorod's golden boy.

Peter the Great stopped in Nizhny Novgorod in 1722 to celebrate his fiftieth birthday and the city's five hundredth. You can bet Peter reveled in the sight of the brisk international trade taking place in and around the city, forming the basis for the future world famous Nizhny Novgorod trade fair. Peter added to all the bustling by ordering warships built on the banks of his "inland port."

During the 1800s Nizhny Novgorod's trade fair became synonymous with the city itself. Merchants from as far as China, Iran, Turkey, and France brought their wares in spring, haggled and bartered during summer, and frequently stayed through autumn to spend their profits on any number of indulgences readily provided on the city's winding back streets. The fair grew to be the largest in Russia, attracting half a million visitors annually. Nizhny Novgorod's population increased tenfold. The appearance of Volga steamships and construction of a railroad to Moscow further bolstered the city's status as Russia's trade capital. A popular saying of the day went, "Petersburg is the head of

Russia, Moscow the heart, and Nizhny Novgorod the pocket."

The late 1800s also ushered in industry. Over one dozen metallurgical plants were built on the outskirts of the city. And, as the story runs with virtually every big Volga city, the combination of capitalism and mass industry eventually gave birth to an unhappy proletarian class which was targeted successfully by Marxists. Only twelve days after Bolsheviks stormed St. Petersburg's Winter Palace in October 1917, they claimed rule in Nizhny Novgorod. Being staunchly opposed to such evils as free enterprise, they promptly put an end to the trade fair.

The city was renamed Gorky in 1932 to honor its famous native son, writer Maxim Gorky (who, by the way, disapproved of the idea). The city's role also changed. It was to become a mecca for Soviet industry. Astoundingly rapid and wide-scale development necessitated expanding Gorky's territory by ten times and quadrupled its population. A 1933 Intourist guidebook boasted, "The ancient fair with its endless Oriental haggling and barter has been replaced by a gigantic new automobile plant!"

Industry and industrial accomplishments became Gorky's source of pride during the Soviet era. The first Russian-produced cars and trucks rolled off Gorky assembly lines. Gorky produced the components for its very own metro system, becoming the first Volga city with a subway. Factories assembled steamships, barges, and railway cars while chemical plants and steel mills gave off steady streams of inspiring smoke.

After World War II (during which Gorky's production capacity played an integral role), plants were set up to develop aerospace hardware and technology. Because of the sensitive nature of these enterprises, Gorky suffered the Cold War distinction of becoming one of the Soviet Union's "closed" cities. And because of its closed status, it was to Gorky that Nobel Laureate Andrey Sakharov was exiled in

1980 after having the audacity to criticize the Soviet Union's invasion of Afghanistan.

Mikhail Gorbachev, in one of the earliest and most symbolic gestures of his *glasnost* policy, freed Sakharov in 1986. Four years later Gorky retained its original name, Nizhny Novgorod. During the Yeltsin era the city has taken a leading role in supporting democracy and, naturally, good old fashioned free enterprise.

ABOUT THE CITY

A population of nearly two million people makes Nizhny Novgorod the third largest city in Russia. Ninety-five percent of the inhabitants are Russian; members of other indigenous Volga ethnic groups such as Mari, Chuvash, and Tatar compose the minority. As can be deduced from its history, the city's main industry is vehicle production. Cars, trucks, trains, riverships—they make them all here. Nizhny Novgorod also serves as Volga River Shipping Company headquarters and home port to a number of passenger ships, so don't be surprised to see members of your ship's crew rejoining family and friends at the port. (And don't be surprised if they return to the ship a bit pickled.) Winter temperatures average below zero centigrade, while in July it is possible to encounter downright balmy days. Native sources refer to the overall climate as "moderately continental," whatever that means.

SIGHTS

As only a few Moscow-St. Petersburg riverships venture as far south as Nizhny Novgorod, it is difficult to predict exactly what sights will constitute your shore excursion. Sights that most local guides tend not to miss include the Nativity Church, the kremlin, the downtown pedestrian street, the art museum, and Andrey Sakharov's house.

A frequent first stop of shore excursions is the charming

Nativity Church (at last check undergoing restoration). Why is this a frequent first stop? Because it stands very close to the river terminal and is really impressive in a birthday cake kind of way. The wealthy Stroganoff family, who monopolized much of Nizhny Novgorod's trade, had the church built at the end of the 17th century. It was completed in 1719. Considered a masterpiece of Russian Baroque, the structure is an extravaganza of frippery, with exterior stucco carved to resemble all kinds of objects, ranging from columns to garlands to grapevines to pomegranates. Every cornice, window, and gable is picked out in white stucco against the red brick of the church's main body. Frosting, lots of frosting. The cupolas are no less striking, sporting psychedelic shingles and other colorful adornments. Inside the church light filtering through the windows on the drums produces a dramatic effect. Naturally there is a gilded iconostasis with some significant icons, but you don't really care about that, do you? During Soviet times, the church housed a crafts organization, which may or may not still be selling its handiwork on the premises. It all depends on how smoothly the transition of church back to Church is going.

Visible from the approach to Nizhny Novgorod, the **kremlin** is a sprawling brick polygon whose walls snake for two kilometers around a hilltop overlooking the junction of the Volga and Oka rivers. The present-day structure dates from the 16th century when Italian architects from Moscow were summoned to design an impregnable fortress. (Invaders had penetrated Nizhny Novgorod's kremlin at least a dozen times already.) The result was walls two meters thick and no less than thirteen towers joining the many angles. Sure enough, the new kremlin withstood subsequent attacks.

Inside the kremlin are four main attractions: a World

War II display-memorial, the Archangel Michael Cathedral, the view of the Volga, and a groovy café. (1) The World War II exhibit is a smattering of war paraphernalia such as tanks and planes and the like. Who knows what it's doing here. (2) The Archangel Michael Cathedral is a 16th century structure beneath which lies the body of national hero Kuzma Minin. Minin died in the 17th century but for some strange reason wasn't brought to his home town until 1964. (3) The Volga panorama at the far end of the kremlin is simply spectacular. (4) The groovy café is located within the tower to your left as you enter the kremlin's main entrance. It's a tri-level affair; don't miss the bottom and top floors!

Nizhny Novgorod's downtown **pedestrian street**, called Bolshaya Pokrovka, is a living relic of the city's ancient past, even though most of its present-day structures date from the 1800s. Lying between Chkalov Square and Gorky Square (both of which feature statues of the men for whom they're named), the thoroughfare has always been the heart of the city. Because only the wealthy could afford to build on such a prime strip of real estate, many of the structures along the street are quite grand and represent a myriad styles, ranging from classical to eclectic to classically boring. The street's most vital attribute, however, is that here you can buy all kinds of souvenirs, loiter in outdoor cafés, and eat street pizza.

The **Nizhny Novgorod Art Museum**, opened in 1896, is one of the oldest galleries in Russia and one of the best. The collection of 6,500 paintings is largely composed of Russian pre-revolutionary works—landscapes, portraits, genre scenes—which were confiscated from local merchants and nobility after the 1917 Revolution. Many of these pieces are accomplished and sensitive renderings of the Russian countryside, character, and soul. There is even some surprisingly inspired Soviet art on display as well.

Sakharov's house is, well, Sakharov's house. Here is where the late champion of human rights passed six years of exile safely out of earshot of the free foreign press. As the place is a bit off the beaten track, not all tours reach it.

THE INSIDE SCOOP
Although it is possible to cover Nizhny Novgorod entirely on foot, the bus tour gets you quickly and easily from one point of interest to the next. It also places you in a strategically central position in the city. Plus it affords you the chance to visit Sakharov's house, which is located some distance from the center. But, as tours don't always go to Sakharov's house, this may be a moot point.

If you have time to spend, you might consider foregoing the ride back to the ship in order to linger downtown. There are enough shops, cafés, and street peddlers on the pedestrian street to entertain you for an afternoon. To get back to the ship, either take tram #1 (which can be caught on an intersecting street approximately in the middle of the pedestrian zone), or, better yet, walk up to Chkalov Square (adjacent to the kremlin) and down the dramatic stone "Volga stairway." This is also a great spot to repose and take in the breathtaking Volga panorama. At the bottom of the stairs follow the back streets in the direction of the port.

For something out of the ordinary, try to find the "beer restaurant" located to the right of the river terminal on an ascending side street. At last check there was no catchy sign in front of the place, but it is recognizable by an out-of-place white faux-marble entrance. The interior is spacious and very chichi, and you can indulge in caviar, grilled sturgeon, and Western cocktails. Rather incongruously, they also have the only dart boards yet seen on the Volga.

GORITSY / KIRILLOV

ORIENTATION

Welcome to Goritsy, home to the Resurrection Convent, visible on the shore. From Goritsy a bus transports you to the town of Kirillov, eight kilometers away. In Kirillov, you tour one of Russia's most famous monasteries, the Monastery of St. Kirill of the White Lake, now a museum. Although most shore excursions concentrate solely on Kirillov, descriptions of both Kirillov and Goritsy follow.

Kirillov: Monastery of St. Kirill of the White Lake

(As a preface to your visit, here is a colorful history of the monastery instead of a written guided tour of its monuments; local guides will furnish you with everything you need to know about the individual edifices.)

At the very end of the 14th century an unusually pious monk named Kirill was appointed archimandrite (abbot) of Moscow's St. Simeon Monastery. Soon thereafter, the sixty year-old man, fed up with the lack of spirituality he saw around him and feeling at the dawn of his life, abandoned his post to "wander around the Russian lands, bow to them, and find a remote region in which to live, as God shall show." Another version of Kirill's story is that one day, while kneeling in prayer in his Moscow monastery, he heard a voice beckoning him to look up. Obeying the voice, he beheld a vision of the Virgin, who commanded him to travel north and found a monastery.

For whatever reason, the old man was soon thereafter spotted digging a cave in the forest atop a point at Lake Siverskoye's edge called Ivanovskaya Hill. Kirill was quite the busy beaver, chopping wood, clearing forest for plowland, and readying a site for a few modest constructions. By the following year Kirill had erected two small churches, a cell for himself, and quarters for those who might want to join him at his retreat. Soon word spread about the holy old man

11.

12.

13.

14.

15.

on the hill, and many pilgrims indeed came to pray with and learn from the recluse monk. Kirill welcomed all, so long as they adopted his ascetic ways. Initial generations of monks were said to boast an average life expectancy of one hundred years due to fasting, living in cold cells, and taking herbs—very potent herbs, one would imagine.

The remote monastic haven rapidly expanded into an influential landowning establishment. It seems that Kirill's asceticism did not extend to his plans for the fledgling monastery itself. He constantly sought to enrich its holdings and did so by aligning himself politically with Muscovy, which had recently annexed the White Lake principality. By allowing the monastery to serve as a northern bulwark for Muscovy, shrewd Kirill gained the favor of the princedom. Such favor meant endowments for his monastery and political influence for himself. By the time of his death, thirty years after founding the monastery, Father Superior Kirill had firmly established the monastery not only as a home for disciplined religious worship, but as a feudal lordship administrating a host of villages and forty separate plots of land, including the serfs attached to those lands.

To the material benefit of the monastery, Kirill's example of exercising religious regimentalism in combination with political adroitness was followed by his successors. Father Superior Trifon in 1433 released deposed Grand Prince Vasily II from a vow not to reseek the Muscovy throne, thereby gaining special treatment for the monastery once Vasily had indeed recaptured the crown. The funds helped erect the monastery's first substantial building, the Assumption Cathedral (still standing, although subsequently altered), completed in 1497. Vasily II's son, Ivan the Great, did not forget the monastery and continued to extend to it great privileges, including free trading rows in Moscow and tax-exempt status on earnings. The monastery was on its way to becoming the country's richest.

Ivan the Great's son Vasily III continued the mutual back-scratching by donating money for the construction of two more cathedrals, the Archangel Gabriel Cathedral and the Church of St. John the Precursor. His gesture was in gratitude for the result of a desperate visit he and his infertile wife made to the monastery to pray for an heir. Their prayers were answered, all right—in the form of a son, the future Ivan the Terrible.

Tsar Ivan, feeling indebted to the monastery for his very conception, continued to lavish it with gifts, donating silver, precious stones, elaborate vestments, and large amounts of money to its ever-growing booty. Much of the money went toward fortifying the monastery with formidable stone walls, parts of which still stand today. Ivan also began using the monastery as a place of exile for his adversaries. Boyars, princes, and even priests were sent to dwell within the mighty white fortress. Their exile, according to rumor, was anything but deprived, consisting of wine-filled soirées in the cells. The indulgent socializing even corrupted the monks, who reportedly were fond of imbibing rather liberally. The final chapter of Ivan's relationship with the monastery consisted of the tsar, suffering from the howling madness that haunted him in his final years, submitting to the monastery a confession containing the names of thousands of people he had ordered killed during his reign. There's no word on whether or not absolution was granted.

The monastery remained loyal to Moscow throughout the ensuing Time of Troubles, assuming the role of bulwark and resisting foreign invaders. Michael Romanov, who emerged from the political tumult to accept the Russian throne, naturally was appreciative of the monastery's service and donated more money. A high-walled "new town" section, the size of which actually surpassed that of the standing monastery, was added to the complex. The beginning of the Romanov dynasty also signaled a change in the monastery's role from country club for exiles to genuine prison for convicted criminals. Russia's Holy Patriarch Nikon even was locked up here after being stripped of his title for being too fanatical. The cell he inhabited afforded a view of a church whose architecture he particularly loathed.

In the middle of the 18th century the monastery reached the apex of its prosperity, with holdings consisting of over 20,000 serfs, 400 villages and associated plots of land, a salt works, and God only knew how much cash.

Descent from the apex later followed. Greed, mismanagement, and moral corruption set in motion the monastery's decline. While political exiles continued to arrive throughout the 18th century and well into the 19th, the fortress itself, no longer of military utility, suffered neglect. The brotherhood began hawking fortifications as well as pieces from the armory collection. Tower chambers were rented out to store salt and vodka. Of the spiritual environment within the monastery at this time, a visitor wrote, "There are no morals, no piety, no cares about anybody or anything. The archimandrite never takes his meals at the refectory, the vice-regent has been on a bender for two months, and the 'brothers'—if they didn't get dead drunk in my face it was only because of a shortage [of spirits]." The pinnacle of debauchery perhaps came after Tsar Alexander II freed the serfs in 1861, causing the archimandrite and brotherhood to sell on the black market some 4,000 valuable manuscripts belonging to the monastery's library in order to remain financially soluble.

During the Civil War that followed the 1917 Revolution the monastery sided with the White Guards in hopes of defeating the atheistic Bolsheviks. When the counter-revolution failed, the Bolsheviks shot the monastery's reigning bishop along with other conspirators. The new government placed the monastery under state control in 1923, calling it a museum of local studies. In 1969 the Soviet government declared the monastery a historical and architectural museum-preserve, ensuring its continuous, albeit lackluster, restoration.

Goritsy: Resurrection Convent

The Resurrection Convent for years was a weed-racked shambles. In 1997, however, active restoration began on its grounds. With luck, it may itself become a worthy tourist destination in the near future.

The convent was founded in 1544 by Moscow Princess Yefrosiniya, wife of Ivan the Great's youngest son, Prince Andrey Staritsky. Yefrosiniya was among a group of boyars who opposed the reigning tsar, Ivan the Terrible, because he sought to diminish boyar influence and privilege. This boyar opposition was secretly plotting to assassinate the tsar and install on the throne Yefrosiniya's son Vladimir. In 1563 Ivan the Terrible uncovered the plot, and heads started to roll. Yefrosiniya was exiled to the very monastery she founded in Goritsy and forced to take the veil under the name of Yevdokiya. Her son Vladimir was executed in Moscow.

Yefrosiniya (now Yevdokiya), with an inkling that her exile might be rather lengthy, arrived at the convent with her servants and embroidery workshop in tow. (Some of the palls she sewed are exhibited in the monastery in Kirillov.) She quickly tired of the monastic life, however, and began appealing regularly to Ivan the Terrible for her pardon and release. The tsar, fed up with the constant pleas, one day sent word to the convent that Yevdokiya was to be freed. He sent to Goritsy a ship, which collected the princess, promptly took her to the middle of the Sheksna River, and drowned her—in accordance with his actual orders.

Princess Yefrosiniya was the first in a long line of women who were compelled to inhabit the convent. Ivan the Terrible, satisfied that the convent satisfactorily had rid him of one troublesome relation, exiled his fourth wife here as well. During the Time of Troubles the daughter of Boris Godunov found herself detained in Goritsy, as did Tsarina Catherine Dolgoruky in 1730 upon the death of her fiancé, fourteen year-old Peter II. The convent regularly hosted 50 to 500 exiled women in addition to its regular sisterhood.

Structures in the complex include three churches: the Resurrection Cathedral (the convent's founding structure built by local craftsmen sponsored by Princess Yefrosiniya in 1544), the early 17th century St. Dmitry Chapel and belfry (built by Ivan the Terrible's fifth wife, Mariya Nagaya, in memory of her son Dmitry, murdered in Uglich in 1591), and the early 19th century Trinity Cathedral (built at the same time as the stone walls enclosing the convent).

THE INSIDE SCOOP
You would be ill-advised to bypass the bus trip to Kirillov, as the Monastery of St. Kirill of the White Lake is the main attraction of this stop. Exhibitions inside the monastery provide an excellent opportunity to scrutinize local handicrafts, including superb examples of famous Vologda lace. While in Kirillov you might want to carve out a few minutes to stray from the monastery into the surrounding countryside or into a few of the town shops. On the main corner, not far from the bus stop, a typical rural bakery sells cookies, candy, and those famed weighty loaves of brown bread.

Occasionally shore excursions forego Kirillov altogether and simply spend the day walking around Goritsy—touring the convent, checking out the statue of a kneeling World War II soldier, chatting up the locals. It's an interesting idea, especially as the convent indeed is worth exploring. The ten-minute trek there, along the shore of the Sheksna, is a small adventure in itself. Once inside the convent, don't be surprised to run into a talkative *babushka* who has been living there since her childhood, over sixty years ago. You'll know her by her charming, weathered countenance.

Take along a Russian speaker if you want to catch her life story.

One last thing. Because the Monastery of St. Kirill of the White Lake in Kirillov is sometimes referred to as the Kirillo-Belozersk Monastery, there has been some misinformation in the past about the exact location of this stop. Despite what you might read in other sources, you are not anywhere near the city of Belozersk, which is located to the north on the west shore of the White Lake.

PETROZAVODSK

ORIENTATION
Petrozavodsk, located fifty-five kilometers across Lake
Onega from Kizhi Island, is the capital of the Karelian
Republic. It is a clean yet nondescript city whose claims to
fame are its origin as an armory foundry, a superb native
dance troop called Kantele, and a Ben and Jerry's ice cream
parlor.

HISTORY
Petrozavodsk stands on the site of a 17th century settlement
called Olonets, an administrative center of a region known
for its iron forging and smithing. With the Northern War
against Sweden getting under way in 1700, Peter the Great
ordered the settlement to establish iron foundries and arma-
ment workshops to supply the military with cannons, can-
nonballs, and assorted weaponry. The first blast furnace of
the Petrovsky Foundry was erected in 1703, and a month
later the first naval cannon was cast. Moscow sent one
hundred top armorers to the plant from the Kremlin Armory
Chamber to assist in the production of war necessities such
as cannons, pistols, muskets, and swords, in addition to war
luxuries like gilded copper cutlass hilts, monogrammed
powder horns, and gilded silver and copper belt buckles.
Demonstrating unsettling versatility, the armory in its spare
time also turned out medical instruments.

Thirteen years after the official defeat of Sweden in
1721, the Petrovsky Foundry closed down. Catherine the
Great reopened it in 1772, as she had committed the military
to a campaign in Turkey and found herself in need of
weapons. In 1777, with Turkish submission achieved,
Catherine renamed the works Alexandrovsky in honor of
the birth of her grandson, future Emperor Alexander I. The
settlement that had grown around the ironworks was renamed *Petrozavodsk*, meaning "Peter's Factory-town."

Eight years later Petrozavodsk became the capital of the Olonets region, presided over by the city's first mayor, an acclaimed Russian poet named G. R. Derzhavin.

In the 19th century activity in Petrozavodsk began to wane, largely due to the lack of railway connection to major centers. With ho-hum wooden houses lining the streets and outdated metallurgy equipment laboring in the Alexandrovsky works, the city assumed a new function as a place of exile for critics of the tsar. Thus another acclaimed poet, Fyodor Glinka, who participated in the 1825 Decembrists' demonstration in St. Petersburg, was installed in Petrozavodsk, albeit amidst slightly less glamorous circumstances than those of his verse-writing predecessor. Glinka's exile here lasted until 1830.

By the beginning of the 20th century Petrozavodsk was well stocked with political exiles leading a fruitless existence in a rather drab town. A contemporary observer commented that the city was "not living, but dozing." A 1916 railroad to Volkhov and Murmansk, built to aid the World War I effort, somewhat restored the city's importance. But it was not until Bolshevik agitators took root in the Alexandrovsky Ironworks in September 1917 and Soviet power was proclaimed in the city the following year that changes occurred. In 1923 Petrozavodsk was named capital of the newly formed Karelian Autonomous Republic. (Although it's an impressive title, the designation carried no power.) The Soviet government converted Petrozavodsk's armaments plants into manufacturers of construction equipment for large-scale civil engineering projects. By 1940 the city had been turned into a Soviet "economic and cultural center," featuring forty-six major industrial enterprises and a host of educational and research institutes.

At the onset of World War II Petrozavodsk transported practically its entire manufacturing operations to a safer but colder region in Siberia. The move turned out to be a shrewd one, as by the end of the war the Soviets had bombed away most of the city trying to force out occupying Finnish troops. With sixty percent of its buildings destroyed, the city resigned itself to a long period of reconstruction after liberation finally was had on 28 June 1944. From the end of war up until the recent dissolution of the Soviet government in 1991, Petrozavodsk lumbered along as the "economic and cultural center" it was designed to be. Admittedly, not much has changed since then, but for a visitor here on a nice day, a walk around the city and along the riverfront can be quite enjoyable.

ABOUT THE CITY
Privileged with a sprawling lakefront aspect, the city of 250,000 people nonetheless is concentrated inland. Typical of the North, the climate is severe, with winters pre-empting autumns and lasting until April. June "white nights" bring twenty hours of sunshine per day as well as warmer temperatures, which peak in July. The population is predominantly employed by various local industries, including mica and lumber processing, furniture and footwear production, prefabricated home construction, and fish canning. The two major businesses, however, are machine building and the city's mainstay, metalworking. A rather anomalous enterprise located here is a Ben and Jerry's ice cream manufacturer. The company originally set its sights on Moscow, but because Moscow's operating tariffs were too high, it quite happily came to Petrozavodsk.

Although local sources mention forty different nationalities represented in the city, one would be hard-pressed to find anyone but Russians, who comprise ninety percent of the population, with Karelians and Finns dividing the remaining ten percent. Nevertheless, the city is considered the heart of Finnish culture in Russia.

Residents of Petrozavodsk decided not to take down their Communist-era monuments or to reinstate pre-Revolutionary street names. The predominant sentiment is that the past cannot and should not be erased by making mere cosmetic changes.

SIGHTS

Although featuring nothing as grand as found in other destinations along the river voyage, Petrozavodsk offers its share of mildly interesting buildings and relatively amusing monuments, most of which will be pointed out to you from behind the windows of a chartered bus—unless you opt to strike out on your own (see "The Inside Scoop").

The park near the river terminal is really the only surviving part of the original settlement, as Catherine the Great was so impressed with it that she decreed it a preserve area. If the statue of Peter the Great seems a little out of place tucked back into the trees here on the city's outskirts, it's because it was moved here from its original prominent location in Round Square to make way for—who else?—Lenin.

Kirov Square is the first main square encountered from the river terminal. It is the former site of the Peter and Paul Cathedral, an intriguing wooden structure built for Peter the Great in 1703 and long since toppled. Providing the intrigue now are metal structures resembling scaffolding planted into the sidewalks bordering the square. These supports formerly displayed Communist Party banners bearing bewildering slogans such as "The Party is the Avante-Garde of the Working Class!" Now they bear advertisements for cigarettes and lotteries—a twist of fate requiring no comment. For further intrigue, behold the sculptural group entitled *Friendship* decorating the pediment of the Neo-Classical Russian Theater; it's about as expressive as Soviet public art gets and it's not bad. Sometimes tour groups are ushered into the Petrozavodsk Museum of Fine Arts, also on the square and also not bad.

Farther along the main street of Marx Prospekt the curiosities continue with a 1960 statue of Marx and Engels sitting on a bench and having a little chat (guess what about). Still farther, opposite the town department store, lies the center of the long city park, "laid out in the 1930s by local residents in their spare time to make Petrozavodsk a green city," according to local literature. More likely the park was laid out during *subotniky*, a uniquely Soviet institution according to which on Saturdays citizens would be "called upon" to volunteer their day off to contribute to public works instead of engaging in dangerous anti-socialist activities like reading Fitzgerald in translation or going to church. Marx Prospekt culminates in Round Square, an oxymoronic name that might be interpreted as epitomizing tsarist as well as communist will toward natural order. Encircling the square (ensquaring the circle?) is a complex of former residences of the original management of the Alexandrovsky Ironworks. At the center of the square stands a granite statue of Lenin sculpted in typically imposing, thoroughly inartistic socialist style. Where the square joins the city park lies the Tomb of the Unknown Soldier; the eternal flame was lit from that of a twin memorial in St. Petersburg's Mars Field.

Back near Kirov Square and across the Lososinka River lies the other side of Petrozavodsk, a more residential region through which tour buses quickly zoom. The Petrozavodsk Museum of Local Studies, in which fine examples of local iron craftsmanship are displayed, is located here. A few blocks away stands the charming, blue-domed Exaltation of the Cross Cathedral, an active church set amongst overgrown trees. The adjacent cemetery, invaded by foliage, produces a somber yet somehow compelling effect.

THE INSIDE SCOOP

You won't hear the ship's staff openly acknowledging it, but there is only one reason for stopping in Petrozavodsk: it is a convenient base from which to make an excursion to famed Kizhi Island. Sure, you'll be beckoned into a bus and given the usual tour of the city, but unless you're the type of person who enthusiastically would take a bus tour of say, Cleveland, the one offered in Petrozavodsk might seem a little uneventful. Of course, if you have a problem with or aversion to walking, the bus has its merits.

However, like virtually every stop along the river, Petrozavodsk can afford the curious traveler a distinct experience. With a repertoire of only marginally interesting sights, the city instead offers an opportunity to glimpse typical Russian daily life. By simply strolling the two kilometer length of Marx Prospekt, which commences at the base of the river terminal and culminates in Round Square, you pass not only the majority of sights listed above, but a number of small shops and cafés within which the occasionally mystifying play of everyday Russian life is acted out. The bar attached to the Finnish Theater can get very lively, especially on weekend nights. By wandering off to the right of Marx Prospekt you encounter still more of what might be called authentic street life. Along Lenin Prospekt there is an interesting art gallery with a cellar café as well as a small park where *shashlik* is often served at outdoor tables.

Whether you stroll Marx Prospekt, cross the Lososinka River to visit the Exaltation of the Cross Cathedral, or explore an entirely different route, this is your chance to indulge in a little of what Russians call *nezateilivoye razvlecheniye*, or "unpretentious fun." Have coffee and pastries in a small café; peruse the bizarre array of items in the town department store; or take care of small errands, as you won't be seeing real civilization for about two days after this, regardless of which direction your ship is heading.

Many ships arrive at Petrozavodsk in the evening and remain docked until morning when the bus tours commence. If you are on board one of these, why not have dinner in town? Recommended restaurants are the Petrovsky, on Marx Prospekt right before Round Square, and the Business Club, located behind the Intourist hotel. You can reach either one by foot or by hiring a taxi at the entry to the pier. The Petrovsky serves very good Russian and Karelian food in the cellar of a former 18th century jail; the Business Club features a charmingly racy cabaret show after dinner (weekends only). For after dinner fun, the river terminal building sometimes hosts a pretty jumpin' disco.

Regarding Ben and Jerry's, some buses make a stop there, some don't. Usually it is decided by a show of hands on the bus. So if your group votes to go eat ice cream and you would rather see sights, change buses. If you *are* craving a waffle cone fix, a bus is your best bet, as the parlor is a bit out of the way.

One last tip. If your group has arranged to see a performance of the renowned Karelian song and dance troupe Kantele, make sure not to miss it. If they have arranged for something else, like a performance by the local ballet company, forget it!

KIZHI ISLAND

ORIENTATION

Situated in the northeast region of Lake Onega, the island of Kizhi is home to an outdoor museum of fascinating edifices of northern wooden architecture, including the remarkable Transfiguration Cathedral.

HISTORY

Accurate documentation of the history of Kizhi is somewhat scarce, largely because of the island's remoteness. The generally accepted version of its early beginnings is that it was an ancient pagan ritual site for northern tribes. Don't be spooked by the phrase "pagan ritual site," for the island's name supposedly was derived from an old Karelian word for "game," suggesting that the atmosphere was more fun-loving than oriented around sinister animal sacrifices. Besides, pagans worship and respect nature rather than a white-bearded white man, so they can't be all that bad. At any rate, despite the presence of the nice pagans, Russian settlers of the 11th century established a natural parish on the island. The area became steadily more populated as southern villagers fled from Mongol-Tatar wrath to the protected northern regions of the Novgorod principality, and as Novgorod serfs escaped to the east to seek an independent life. With an abundance of fish, game, and fertile soil, the island and its surroundings continued to attract hardy settlers throughout the 12th and 13th centuries.

In 1478 Ivan the Great annexed Novgorod to Muscovy. With a fondness for centralizing territory that made him the father of Russian bureaucracy, Ivan began exacting taxes on the Kizhi *pogost*, an "administrative unit" usually centered around a church and cemetery. By the next century the territory of the *pogost* extended for 40 kilometers around the island and included 130 small villages. At this time thirteen villages and two churches stood on Kizhi itself.

During the unstable Time of Troubles the *pogost* alternately was at the mercy of Poles, Lithuanians, and Swedes, all of whom were all poised to overrun the country. Kizhi villagers dispersed into the countryside. When they returned after relative order was restored, they found themselves acting as border guards on an island-cum-defense-post, a role they relished not. When Peter the Great decided to put an end to the Swedish threat once and for all, he "summoned" peasants from Kizhi to work in his newly established armory plant in Petrozavodsk. For all practical purposes Russia had won the war by 1709, and the Transfiguration Cathedral was erected on Kizhi in 1714 partly in commemoration of the victory. The Intercession Church, built fifty years later, was the last symbol of flourishing on the island. As increasing numbers of craftsmen left Kizhi to work in St. Petersburg, the island entered a period of decline in the 19th century from which it never recovered.

One of the first acts of the Bolshevik government was to issue a conservation decree mandating that certain antique wooden buildings of the Onega region be preserved because they "represent the results of genuinely proletarian creativity, showing how during times of persecution and oppression our people were able to convincingly portray their beliefs, hopes, and aspirations." Its rhetoric aside, the decree saved the two extraordinary churches standing on Kizhi Island. Moreover it resulted ultimately in the island's acquisition of examples of traditional architecture from around the Onega region. An outdoor museum was thus formed; it opened in 1966.

ABOUT THE ISLAND
Kizhi is small and narrow, measuring approximately six kilometers by one kilometer. Its north-central location in Lake Onega makes for misty early mornings and dazzling dawns in summer; otherwise, its climate is comparable to Petrozavodsk's.

Perhaps the most intriguing facets of the island itself are the colorful myths surrounding it. A visit to the island is thought to improve one's life by excising diseases, by revealing the keys to personal happiness, and by bringing business success. More specifically,

– Dental problems are said to be rectified by rubbing against the small Archangel Michael Chapel, the logs of which actually have been visibly worn by hopefuls. Exactly which part of the body is to be rubbed is not clear, but if you return to the ship with splinters in your gums, you probably deserve the derision you'll receive.

– Taking a bath on the island is supposed to ensure one of marriage within a year. Whether or not marriage is considered one of the "keys to personal happiness" is also not clear. Oh, and in order for the bath to work it must be drawn from a mixture of herbs and *kvas* (a beverage made from fermented dark bread), and it must be placed under a spell by a witch.

– Business success is virtually guaranteed upon sighting mermaids combing their locks on the footbridge near the small wooden bathhouse.

Additionally, residents of Kizhi are said to allow the island's indigenous snakes to slither freely through their homes, as the creatures are believed to indicate fields of the earth's kinetic energy, thereby showing the inhabitants how to best arrange their furniture, where to hang pictures, etc. The upholding of this tradition has not recently been verified.

SIGHTS

Officially called the State Historical, Architectural and Ethnographic Preserve of Kizhi, the collection of structures planted predominantly along the southern tip of the island consists of churches, chapels, bell towers, peasant houses, granaries, barns, windmills, and bathhouses—all brought from around the Onega region to collectively illustrate the styles of architecture common to the Russian North. The focal point, referred to as the "Kizhi Ensemble," comprises the awe-inspiring Transfiguration Cathedral, the neighboring Intercession Church, and the bell tower between the two, all of which are enclosed by a stone and wood fortification. The two churches of the ensemble are the only structures originally built on the island.

Thirty thousand shingles on twenty-two separate cupolas situated on five tiers compose the ascending nest that is the **Transfiguration Cathedral**, built in 1714. It is certainly an impressive structure, considering it was built as a mere summer church and without nails. (The nails visible today are from restoration executed in the 1960's.) It is even more impressive if you believe the popular legend that it was built by one man with one tool, an ax. Supposedly, upon affixing the final shingle, the master carpenter, named Nestor, hurled his ax into Lake Onega, proclaiming, "*Ne bylo, net i ne budet takoi*," meaning "There never was, nor will there ever be such!" What he probably meant was that there never was, nor will there ever be such a pain in the rear end to build.

The shingles are made of aspen wood, which resists weathering fairly well, responds to aging very well, and is capable of reflecting a myriad magical hues. Midday sunshine makes them shimmer like silver, while the light of dawn or dusk turns them a rich purple. Unfortunately the circular interior of the cathedral, originally featuring a gilded iconostasis, has been closed for the last several years due to preservation bureaucracy. Rumor has it that the bureaucracy includes debate over facing the entire structure with planks to protect it from deterioration. One can only hope a more rational plan will be adopted.

The interior of the nearby **Intercession Church** is open to visitors and houses icons from its closed neighbor. Built in 1764 as a winter church, its roof too was constructed without nails. Some historians argue that the structure was intended to support a gabled roof, but being left unfinished for a time, it was given a flat roof with nine shingled cupolas to better complement the Transfiguration Cathedral. Considering the church's irregular proportions, the theory is quite plausible. But whether or not the building is in architectural harmony with itself and/or its awesome neighbor is up to you to decide. (Whether or not it's important also is up to you to decide.)

The 1874 **bell tower**, which until recently was open for climbing, completes the ensemble of fir, pine, and aspen called by one observer "an original song in wood."

Other significant structures through and around which you will be dutifully conducted are the modest Chapel of the Resurrection of Lazarus (built in 1391, making it the oldest standing wooden church in Russia), the Chapel of the Archangel Michael (with its healing powers), and a series of authentic peasant houses and farm structures.

THE INSIDE SCOOP

This is a pretty cut and dried scene. You're on a small island with a lot of different examples of ancient northern architecture and you have well-informed local guides (actually they boat over from Petrozavodsk) to show and tell you everything you ever wanted to know about the place. However, if while going on and on about the fairy tale appearance of the buildings, your guide's English speech patterns start to cause you to drift off into your own never-never land, it might be time to break away and take in the refreshing Kizhi countryside. Even if you stick with the tour for its duration, you should have some time left for a little walk.

Following any of the dirt trails away from the main body of the outdoor museum will lead you to more pastoral settings. You'll traverse some rolling hills and pass the island's small cemetery, an overgrown hodge-podge of colorful and uniquely assembled grave sites that would strike envy into the heart of a modern-day mixed-media artist. The well-prepared might even make a modest picnic on one of the hilltops, which command exhilarating views of the island and lake. Those in the mood for adventure might wander through some of the island's small villages, while fitness-oriented folks feeling a bit constrained by shipboard aerobics should be able to squeeze in an extremely satisfying jog. (And think of how chic you'll sound back home—"Mmm, yes, I believe it was in '97 or '98, while I was taking a morning jog around Kizhi Island in Karelia...")

Wherever you venture, remember to take along mosquito repellent to combat the bloodsucking helicopters native to the island and to watch out for the poisonous snakes that guides will tell you are rampant. (We think they just want to keep tourists from venturing out on their own and missing the boat.) As for the big restaurant near the landing pier, it hasn't been open in years.

VALAAM ISLAND
–not visited by all ships–

ORIENTATION
Valaam is the main island of a rugged archipelago tucked into the northeasternmost region of Lake Ladoga. The island constitutes a unique and diverse northern natural preserve and is home to one of the Russian Orthodox Church's most sacred monasteries.

HISTORY
The story of Valaam is inextricably linked to the saga of its Transfiguration Monastery, the centerpiece of a necklace of religious edifices that at one time numbered twenty-three churches and nineteen chapels adorning Valaam and the surrounding islands. Legend tells that two Greek monks, Herman and Sergius, founded the monastery in the year 992, thereby establishing the most northwest outpost of the Orthodox Church. When Herman and Sergius died, their remains defied decomposition, earning the monks canonization. Their monastery, however, allegedly was not as lucky and was completely destroyed in 1163.

The better documented and more believable version of the monastery's founding is that it sprung up in 1329 as a base for missionaries plying their trade in Karelia.

Although historians argue over whether or not the structure originally was fortified, they agree that the island was the sight of repeated confrontations between the Swedish kingdom and Novgorod principality. In fact, notwithstanding a period of relative flourishing from the mid-14th to the mid-15th century, the monastery was ravaged periodically by the Swedes until Peter the Great subdued them finally in the early 18th century. In 1715 Peter himself visited Valaam, ordering the restoration and protection of the monastery.

The island thereafter developed into a regional economic center with international spiritual influence. Valaam missionaries ventured as far as the Aleutian Islands and Alaska to seed Orthodox beliefs. In 1822 the monastery was bestowed with "first class" status (whatever that means). A few decades later, professional architects of the "Russian Style" school began restoring and adding to the monastery complex. Wealthy visitors from St. Petersburg, reaching the island on newly opened water routes in 1843, contributed to the revival. By the end of the century nine new *sketes*, or subsidiary monasteries, had been constructed on and around the island. The monastery, at this time one of the wealthiest in the country, found itself at the head of its own mini-state, operating factories and developing agriculture.

During this period of revival Valaam also became a popular holiday destination. Visiting during summers, Orthodox pilgrims were joined by notable artists, writers, and scientists seeking spiritual refreshment. Famous Russian painters Kuindzhi, Shishkin, and Rerikh all spent time on the island, as did the composer Tchaikovsky, who recuperated here from a nervous breakdown inflicted by the pressure of writing his first symphony.

While visitors were busy seeking inspiration, monks inhabiting the outlying *sketes* observed a rather stoic regime, which included a strict prohibition on the presence of women. The prohibition was lifted, however, one day per year. (And what a day that likely was.) The monastic island lifestyle also attracted large numbers of *bogomoltsy*, a regiment of monks dedicated to praying for the sovereign.

In 1917, when Lenin and Trotsky summarily excused Russia from World War I, Valaam became the domain of Finland. The monastery continued to thrive. By 1938 the population of nearly 200 monks maintained a large-capacity hostel, a candle manufactory, a forge, a complex of art studios and workshops, and a shipyard. In addition they engaged in fishing, agriculture, and horticulture.

Two years later, however, the monks found themselves scurrying en masse to mainland Finland when Stalin regained the island for the atheistic Soviet Union in 1940. In Finland the monks founded the New Valaamo Monastery to house the icons, vestments, and 30,000-volume Slavonic library with which they wisely absconded. Rumor has it they even took with them the remains of the monastery's legendary founders, St. Herman and St. Sergius. Back on Valaam, the Soviets closed the Transfiguration Monastery, shoed away any remaining monks, and opened a naval academy.

In keeping with the trend induced by *perestroika*, the government in 1989 returned several Valaam structures to the Orthodox Church. Soon thereafter the first six monks of a new era arrived on the island. In summer of 1992 President Boris Yeltsin was joined on the island by Holy Patriarch of Russia Alexiy II to sign a decree restoring the entire monastery complex to the Church. The government, however, neglected to address the fate of the secular population of 500 residents who had taken up quarters in the monastery's apartments since the 1950s, thus sparking volatile relations between the monks and workers. At last account the two factions were still battling over the right to inhabit the monastery grounds.

ABOUT THE ISLAND

Occupying 36 square kilometers over Lake Ladoga's greatest depths of 230 meters, the Valaam archipelago consists of one main island and fifty smaller ones, all made up of granite and diabase. The largest island, Valaam, occupies 28 square kilometers. It is home to the greatest variety of flora, largely due to the horticultural efforts of monks over the centuries. Coniferous forest covers the island, although alleys of fir and larch trees as well as groves of cedar, oak, and apple trees stand amidst stretches of meadows. In all, over 460 varieties of plantlife take root in the island.

Although wildlife enthusiasts would be lucky to spot the elk, fox, hare, and ermine that inhabit the remoter areas, birdwatchers might catch sight of finches, siskins, thrushes, and chiff-chaffs. From the shores, gulls and even seals can be spied. Valaam is a natural wildlife preserve, which means that nothing on the island should be killed—including the ubiquitous monster-size mosquitoes that relish tourist blood.

SIGHTS
The ship approaches Valaam from the southwest, hooking around a few small islands and then gliding into Nikon's Bay, named after the fanatical 17th century patriarch of Russia. Anchor is cast at the base of a hill upon which stands one of Valaam's small secluded mini-monasteries, the **Resurrection Skete**. The hill itself is called New Jerusalem, a tribute to one of the far-off destinations of pilgrimage to which Valaam monks have ventured. Because the island was returned to the Church only in 1992 most restoration and religious activity is conducted at the main Transfiguration Cathedral; the outlying sketes are still deserted. Entertaining local tour guides usually make the most of your visit to the *skete*, however, also taking you for a short walk to the nearby Assumption Church of the Gethsemane Skete, also uninhabited.

Valaam's main attraction, the Transfiguration Monastery, is not visited by most shore excursions. For information on how to get to it, see "The Inside Scoop."

THE INSIDE SCOOP
Passengers tend to be divided over whether or not the excursion to Valaam Island is worthwhile. Some would not hear of missing the natural beauty that graces the environs of one of Russia's most sacred monasteries. Others easily could forego the round trip boat ride to the northernmost reach of oceanlike Lake Ladoga just to take a tour of a few

deserted and remote religious compounds. If truth be told, the tour typically offered to tourists on Valaam is more or less a waste of time because it completely neglects the two things that make Valaam an unforgettable destination: the extraordinary natural setting of the island and the famous Transfiguration Monastery. Adventurous visitors, however, can see these things on their own, usually without even missing the organized tour. Some ships actually do arrange a chartered boat ride to the Transfiguration Monastery; if you are a passenger of such a ship, then you may consider yourself blessed and disregard the diatribe above and directions below.

On your own there are essentially three ways to reach the Transfiguration Monastery, located to the northeast of Nikon's Bay. One is simply to walk along the main dirt road lying at the top of the sloping embankment. After immediately coming to the colorful yet uninspired Assumption Church, simply continue along the road without diverting. The six kilometer trek to the monastery takes about 45 minutes. The second possibility is to hire a motorboat near the passenger pier. You will be conducted through a narrow bay, out into Lake Ladoga, and back through a picturesque straight to Monastery Bay, where the main cathedral bell tower submits an awesome welcome. The third variant is to stow away on a chartered boat taking passengers from another rivership to the monastery. A combination of boating and walking is perhaps the ideal way to see the most of the island within the allotted time. Boat rides sometimes can be negotiated (or infiltrated) at the monastery as well. Along the road you can always flag down a car or truck to get you to or from the monastery more quickly.

You approach the monastery by climbing sixty-two granite steps to an outlying yard. To the right of the footpath stands the tiny Tsar's Chapel, commemorating the visit of Alexander II in 1858. To the left stands an obelisk paying tribute to the visit of Peter the Great. The path leads through an archway known as the Holy Gates, the main entrance to the monastery. The arch supports the Church of Peter and Paul above, crowned by a single cupola. The Transfiguration Cathedral, built in 1887 on the site of earlier cathedrals, is topped with five azure domes and adjoined by a seventy meter-high belfry containing a colossal sixteen ton bell that sounds the hour. Decaying frescoes, most of which are reproductions of the work of 19th century artist Gustave Dore, cover the interior walls. Above the altar is a reproduction of Leonardo's *Last Supper*.

The state of restoration will determine which parts of the monastery you can visit. If possible, try climbing the belfry for a breathtaking panorama of the island. If you're feeling relaxed or in need of refreshment, seek out one of the nearby cafés before heading back.

ST. PETERSBURG

ORIENTATION
Welcome to St. Petersburg turned Petrograd turned Leningrad turned St. Petersburg once again. Located on the Finnish Bay of the Baltic Sea, the second largest city in Russia at times appears thoroughly Westernized, breathtakingly romantic, and refreshingly progressive, yet can also reveal an enigmatic soul, charmless filth, and frustrating backwardness.

HISTORY
In keeping with the megalomania inherent to Russia's most reputed rulers, Peter the Great hiked out to a marshy, mosquito-infested island in the delta of the Neva River on 16 May 1703, decided the location would be a perfect port for his future navy, cut two strips of soil from the earth, laid them in the shape of a cross, and pronounced, "Here there shall be a city." In keeping with the ruthlessness inherent to Russia's most reputed rulers, he forced Swedish prisoners as well as destitutes from his own country to dredge the area, dig out a system of canals, and lay foundations for initial structures. In keeping with the tyranny inherent to Russia's most reputed rulers, the tsar compelled his subjects to inhabit the place.

So goes the founding of St. Petersburg, a city "built on bones," a "window on the West," a thoroughly unique European metropolis by virtue of its being preconceived by a unified vision and then executed according to that vision. In actuality Peter's first concern was building a fortress to aid his Northern War effort, already three years under way. He also wanted to consolidate a major trade route through the Baltic Sea to Russia's inland waterways. Perhaps most important, he wanted to be as close to Europe as possible, for after his eye-opening European tour of 1697 he decided he liked what was going on there more than what was happening in his homeland. But Peter could only be a tsar in Russia, so he decided to bring the West to him—and to his chagrined compatriots.

Despite laborers having to carry dirt away in their shirts and routinely dropping dead from malaria, scurvy, or starvation, the first wooden structures of the new city were erected on *Zayachiy ostrov* ("Hare's Island") some five months after Peter's ground-breaking. These buildings, including fortifications and a church, formed the Peter and Paul Fortress, the city's first structural ensemble, where Peter's tomb today rests.

Despite the ongoing war with Sweden, Peter confidently urged on development. Workers erected a military outpost on Kronstadt Island in the very mouth of the Neva, a handful of residences and civic structures on nearby Petrograd Island, and the Admiralty naval base on the mainland. Russia then defeated the Swedes in the war's decisive battle at Poltava in the Ukraine in 1709. Although on paper the war lasted another eleven years, for all practical purposes it was over, prompting Peter to boast, "Now the final stone has been laid on the foundation of St. Petersburg." Construction pressed on with a fury. Every inhabitant of the city was obliged to provide 100 stones per year to aid such projects as laying the main street, later called Nevsky Prospekt. In 1710 the imperial family moved to St. Petersburg from Moscow, bringing with them most government institutions.

In 1712 Peter declared St. Petersburg the new capital of Russia. To the Moscow aristocracy and merchant class the decree was horrifying—not so much because they lost the capital, but because they feared they would be induced to inhabit the uncivilized northern jungle of which their robust sovereign was so fond. And they were right. Given a choice between relocating or losing their heads, boyars and merchants reluctantly moved to the young city where they were obliged to build large dwellings at their own expense. They were joined by 40,000 masons who had flocked to the city owing to Peter's decree forbidding building in stone anywhere but St. Petersburg. Work camps larger than the city itself sprung up to accommodate the huge influx of serfs and prisoners compelled to do the necessary hard labor. Life in the fledgling city was about as agreeable as most had expected. Floods routinely plagued the islands and wolves roamed free after dark. Nevertheless, by the time of Peter's death in 1725 close to 100,000 people inhabited the city and ninety percent of Russia's foreign trade passed through it.

Although during Peter's life the fortress-capital he constructed never got the chance to prove itself in battle, it was destined to become the center of Western culture that he envisioned. Aside from Peter's grandson, Peter II, who moved the imperial court to Moscow for a couple of years before dying of smallpox in 1730, all future monarchs remained faithful to Peter's dream, ruling happily from the aristocratic European setting of St. Petersburg, implicitly snubbing Moscow and the rest of Russia in the process.

The first great strides towards firmly establishing the city as a Western showcase were made by Empress Elizabeth (1741-61). Despite being as rambunctious as her father, Peter the Great, and being as indulgent as Imelda Marcos (Elizabeth is said to have owned 15,000 dresses), the empress established the St. Petersburg Academy of Arts and commissioned Italian architect Rastrelli to build the Winter Palace and Smolny Cathedral.

A brief power struggle followed Elizabeth's death in 1761, with the German-born wife of Elizabeth's nephew Peter emerging to solidify her status as autocratix in 1762. Better known as Catherine the Great, she grabbed the Westernizing torch and ran with it. French became the official language of the court, Enlightenment ideas pervaded philosophical as well as social circles, and freedom of expression in arts and literature was encouraged (although in practice not fully tolerated). In the estimation of 19th century French traveler the Marquis de Custine, the Empress Catherine "knew nothing of the arts or of poetry," yet she nonetheless established the foundation of the Hermitage's extraordinary artwork holdings by purchasing several private European collections. By the time of Catherine's death in 1796 the city of St. Petersburg was heralded as one of Europe's grandest capitals, with a court of famed splendor and an appearance considered by some as consisting of regal architectural masterpieces, while considered by others, like Custine, as comprising "shapeless monuments copied from the models of antiquity."

Issues of architectural originality aside, there was no doubt that by the 19th century St. Petersburg had succeeded in becoming the administrative and cultural center of the Russian Empire. The city's population of nearly 600,000 was double that of the forgotten former capital, Moscow. Despite increasing despotism emanating from the Winter Palace, the Golden Age of Russian literature was born in St. Petersburg as novelists Dostoyevsky and Turgenev embarked on literary careers and poets Pushkin and Lermontov scribed their best verses before being killed in duels.

Its geographical orientation, however, continued to bring the city peril. Devastating floods in 1824, which swelled the Neva four meters over its normal level, drowned thousands of people and ruined countless buildings. Several geographically unrelated events, such as the Napoleonic invasion in 1812, the Decembrists' revolt in 1825, and a series of serf uprisings, put the monarchy on the defensive, which meant a tightening of the reigns on the citizenry. Although Alexander II emancipated the serfs in 1861, emerging radical groups such as Populists and Nihilists remained dissatisfied with the autocratic system and began stirring up widespread political discontent. By the 1880s government officials, including the tsar, had become common targets for terrorist attacks. Alexander II didn't mind his back closely enough and was killed by a bomb in 1881 at the site of the present-day mosaic-covered Savior on the Blood Cathedral. By the end of the century factories had sprung up in the suburbs of St. Petersburg, drawing a large urban working class to the troubled capital. As the 20th century drew near, grumbling directed at the outdated and out-of-touch monarchy grew steadily louder.

On 9 January 1905 a peaceful congregation of 150,000 striking workers and families marched to Palace Square to hand Tsar Nicholas II a petition demanding basic civil rights and labor laws. Nicholas, not grasping the importance of the demonstration, was off spending the day with his family at their beloved royal retreat in Tsarskoye Selo (called Pushkin today). In the tsar's absence edgy troops opened fire on the crowd, killing thousands of unarmed citizens, including children. The confrontation became known as Bloody Sunday and put the writing on the wall for the doomed monarchy. Insulated from reality by his handlers throughout his reign, Nicholas wrote in his diary, "9 January 1905. A difficult day! In Petersburg there were serious disturbances."

At the start of World War I in 1914 St. Petersburg shirked its German-sounding name and became Petrograd, a Russified version of the original. The war went badly for Russia from the outset, only intensifying unrest in the capital. That Nicholas had a domineering German wife who was politically influenced by a notoriously debauched religious charlatan named Rasputin didn't help the tsar's popularity. After mass strikes and demonstrations in anarchic Petrograd in February 1917, the tsar abdicated on 2 March 1917.

The provisional government that set up shop in the Winter Palace failed to satisfy anyone, including Bolsheviks led by Lenin and Trotsky. Bearing arms, the Bolsheviks took to the streets of Petrograd on 24 October 1917, storming the Winter Palace and establishing a new government. The political maneuvering that followed is rather involved; suffice it to say that the Bolsheviks and Lenin proved not to be as dedicated to the peoples' will as they originally claimed, disbanding Russia's first democratically elected Constituent Assembly and seizing absolute power by force. Bloody civil war raged throughout the country for the next several years.

As for Petrograd, the city lost its clout when Lenin moved the capital back to safer ground in Moscow after having given away the Baltic States as part of the 1918 Treaty of Brest. By 1920 two-thirds of Petrograd's population had vacated the former capital. Upon Lenin's death in 1924 the city was renamed Leningrad, which bothered no one, as lifelong residents had always called the city "Piter" anyway.

In the 1930s the more paranoid Josef Stalin became, the emptier became Leningrad. He ruthlessly purged the city of its military and political officials as well as other "threatening individuals." ("Purge," by the way, is a nice word for remove-and-kill.) Stalin also included Leningrad in his push for Russia's mass industrialization, ordering more factories set up in its suburbs. However, because Stalin basically disliked Leningrad he inadvertently saved it from suffering the same face lift that converted once mystically beautiful Moscow into a vast wasteland of concrete. The raving Georgian actually thought he was depriving Leningrad of privilege by not tearing down its historic architecture. Although no one admires Stalin, save a handful of disillusioned loonies, citizens of St. Petersburg today are in his debt for keeping his grubby hands off their lovely city.

Rumor has it, however, that the harrowing siege of Leningrad during World War II might have been more or less "allowed" by Stalin, who saw the opportunity to save on

TNT by letting the Germans desecrate the city for him. Whether or not the rumor is accurate, there is no disputing that the siege of Leningrad, known as "900 Days" (actually 872), was among the most horrific in history. From September 1941 to January 1944 the city was cut off from steady supplies of food, water, gas, and electricity. Occasionally bread and ammunition were brought in by trucks that drove across the ice of Lake Ladoga's "Road of Life." Although the Ladoga route also enabled the evacuation of one million people, another one million Leningraders perished. During the unusually harsh winter of 1942 alone, 4,000 people per day died of starvation or cold. People falling dead on the sidewalks and corpses lying in the street were common sights. Cats and rats were not common sights, for reasons to be inferred. Miraculously the city persevered, even retaining a semblance of cultural life by organizing makeshift theaters and concerts throughout the blockade.

Although Leningrad received the best of the country's foodstuffs for a period after the war in gratitude for its grit, it was thanked by Stalin by being purged again in 1947-53. Growing more and more paranoid, especially about the powerful solidarity that the war experience had created among Leningraders, Stalin put on show trials in which "traitors" confessed to fabricated crimes before being executed or sent off to perish in the GULAG. The steady depletion of the population did not exactly aid the Herculean task of rebuilding the city, which had lost one-third of its structures during the war. The death of Stalin in 1953 finally allowed Leningrad some breathing room to rebuild, repopulate, and enjoy the "thaw" of the Khrushchev years. Not until the 1960s did the city's population reach pre-World War II levels.

During the humdrum Brezhnev era the city bided its time, slowly wasting away amidst Soviet self-deception like the rest of Russia. Moscow was clearly the center of the country, although innovations in music, art, and literature continued to pour forth from more cultural Leningrad. The city welcomed Mikhail Gorbachev's *perestroika* and *glasnost*, electing a progressive mayor, Anatoly Sobchak, in 1990. The following year the city voted to change its name back to St. Petersburg, a gesture symbolic of the type of future the populace would like to embrace.

ABOUT THE CITY

St. Petersburg and Moscow have cultivated a historic rivalry similar to that between San Francisco and Los Angeles. Muscovites consider Leningraders (as they still call St. Petersburg residents) rather snobbish, which is probably accurate, as citizens of St. Petersburg regard inhabitants of Moscow merely with pity.

Tsar Nicholas I once remarked that "St. Petersburg is Russian, but it is not Russia." Indeed the unique "Petersburg soul" is a frequently invoked distinction. If truth be told, however, the only noticeably distinguishing trait of modern day St. Petersburg residents is a peculiar kind of arrogance that, as John Nicolson mentions in *The Other St. Petersburg* (1994), makes them consider "ambition as something you catch if you spend too much time in Moscow."

But there certainly is something special about a city and a people that bask in soft northern light for twenty-four hours a day in summer and endures long, foreboding nights in winter. Occupying an area of 600 square kilometers, the city spreads itself on 42 separate islands interlaced with close to 70 canals and rivers spanned by some 300 bridges. Referred to as the "Venice of the North" (but resembling Venice only in the most generous of imaginations), the city lies on the same latitude as Alaska, yet its winter climate remains milder than Moscow's due to warming Atlantic air masses crossing the Baltic Sea.

The city itself is considered a museum of architecture,

boasting over 200 stunning palaces and monuments, typically representing Baroque or Neo-Classical styles. For cultural stimulation the population of almost five million chooses from over 50 museums, 20 theaters and concert halls, 60 stadiums, and 4,500 libraries. For recreation inhabitants repair to *dachas* in the Karelian isthmus or to the immaculate country palaces in the immediate environs. Industries include shipbuilding, heavy engineering, printing, brewing, textiles, electronics, and tourism.

SIGHTS

Usually docking at St. Petersburg for only two days, ships provide shore excursions that concentrate on a few major sights in addition to one of the country palaces. Brief synopses of the routinely visited attractions are here listed. Additional sightseeing ideas are suggested in "The Inside Scoop."

Hermitage Museum

The Hermitage is the mother of all art museums. It boasts the biggest collection of artwork and antiquities in the world. In terms of sheer size and scope, it has only three rivals: the Louvre in Paris, the Prado in Madrid, the Met in New York. In terms of amenities like smart cafés and museum shops, it has no rivals whatsoever, as it is devoid of any such modern comforts. Unlike those other museums, all you can do here is look at poorly lit art masterpieces. The holdings of the collection include some 12,000 sculptures, 15,000 paintings, 225,000 works of applied art, and over 600,000 drawings and prints. Spanning 400 of the Winter Palace's 1,057 rooms, the exhibition is made up of 2.8 million display pieces, and it is said that to spend a few moments at each one would require nine years. More remarkable is that only a small percentage of the museum's entire collection is on view at any given time.

Like the city in which it is displayed, the Hermitage art

collection was started by Peter the Great, who picked up a few Dutch maritime scenes while visiting Holland in 1697, hanging them in his country palace at Peterhoff. Later, after acquiring more significant works, like a canvas by Rembrandt and a statue of Aphrodite, Peter began displaying the art in the Winter Palace (an earlier and much more modest version than the present one), likely having no idea what he was germinating. Catherine the Great took Peter's cue and became the collection's greatest patron, in spite of her limited knowledge of the arts. Figuring that anyone who corresponds with Voltaire and Diderot ought to own some impressive art too, Catherine first bought a collection of 250 Dutch and Flemish paintings from a Berlin merchant who was short of cash. She purchased 600 more paintings from Count Brühl of Saxony in addition to procuring substantial portions of other European collections. Whenever her ambassadors traveled abroad, Catherine bade them to attend art auctions and buy, buy, buy!

Although no one person after Catherine went quite as bonkers over building the collection, Tsar Alexander I kept the imperial art-amassing tradition alive by relieving Napoleon's wife Josephine of her entire art collection after France's defeat in 1814. Nicholas I, not to be outdone, bought the collection of Napoleon's stepdaughter. After the 1917 Revolution the Bolsheviks consolidated the museum's holdings by confiscating all of Russia's privately owned art collections. Only Stalin had the chutzpah to take from the collection, selling off a suite of Rembrandts and some Fabergé eggs for foreign currency.

The present-day museum complex, officially called the State Hermitage, comprises five structures: the Winter Palace, the Small Hermitage, the New Hermitage, the Old Hermitage, and the Hermitage Theater. All buildings but the theater contain exhibits of the museum. The Small Hermitage and Old Hermitage were the first additions to the

Winter Palace intended primarily to house artwork. They were constructed in 1764-87 by order of Catherine the Great. The New Hermitage was commissioned by Nicholas I in 1839.

When the New Hermitage was completed in 1852 a limited public for the first time was allowed to view the collection. Prior to that, it had existed solely for imperial enjoyment, prompting Catherine to once write in a letter, "All this is admired by mice and myself." The Bolsheviks, after looting and vandalizing the Winter Palace in 1917, eventually cleaned up their mess, filled it with paintings, and opened its doors to the public as the main exhibition space of the Hermitage Museum.

While inside the Hermitage, determining which structure is which can be rather difficult. It really makes little difference, as your head will be spinning from the dizzying array of artwork anyway. Western European painting is presented with extreme breadth from the 13th century through the Renaissance up to Post-Impressionism. Impressionistic painting in fact is one of the strong points of the museum due to the collecting efforts of two undaunted Russian aristocratic art patrons named Shchukin and Morozov. The two savvy art collectors also befriended and supported Matisse and Picasso when the rest of Europe was too squeamish, so the galleries are packed with the works of those two great heroes in addition to all the offerings of Renoir, Monet, Pissarro, and others. If surveying canvases by hero artists isn't your scene, however, the Winter Palace's gorgeous state rooms are sure to impress with their regal spaciousness, delightful color schemes, and opulent adornment. Also, don't forget the rooms full of prehistoric, Egyptian, Oriental, and Classical antiquities, not to mention exciting temporary exhibitions. There is no question that the place is just too darn big. But you're in St. Petersburg, so you gotta go. Good luck.

St. Isaac's Cathedral

From the outside, St. Isaac's looks exactly like the fourth largest domed cathedral in the world that it is. Austerely regal by day and ominously imposing by night, the monstrous structure took forty years to build (1818-1858). The architect, a Frenchman named Montferrand, submitted twenty-four different plans in order to garner the commission. He labored his entire life on the project, redesigning as the structure's shortcomings or the tsar's will periodically manifested. Just to prepare for the project an army of serfs laid 20,000 tree trunks to firm the site, and special ships and railways were built to haul granite pillars from Finland. By the time the 30,000-ton edifice was completed, building costs had exceeded by ten times those of the Winter Palace. Montferrand, by the way, was so consumed by the project that he expired one month after he witnessed its completion. When his wife requested that he be buried within his beloved chef-d'œuvre, she was promptly rebuked and told to ship the body of her non-Orthodox hubby back to France.

Although the cathedral's gray marble exterior adorned with colonnades of red granite, gold-covered domes, and bronze statues, is striking (albeit tarnished), its interior is the main attraction. Fourteen varieties of marble, generous touches of jasper, malachite, and gilded stucco, plentiful frescoes, mosaics, and murals, in addition to a carved white marble iconostasis in front of a sanctuary illuminated by stained glass (an unusual feature in an Orthodox church) make for one of the most spectacular interior spaces of any building anywhere. Moreover, due to painstaking renovation, it is absolutely immaculate; the full saturation of employed colors is vibrantly alive.

And a visit to St. Isaac's is not complete without hiking up to the colonnade surrounding the drum of the dome to behold an unrivaled panorama of the entire city. Acrophobes and claustrophobes not recommended.

Peter and Paul Fortress

In 1703 Peter the Great laid the first stone of the Peter and Paul Fortress, an outpost on tiny Hare's Island designed to defend against the Swedes. Although Peter defeated the Swedes without the aid of the fortress, its construction signaled the founding of St. Petersburg. Within five months of ground-breaking, a wooden fortress and church had been erected. By the time it was completed, one year after Peter's death in 1725, the ensemble had been rebuilt in stone and was protected by 12 meter-thick walls supporting some 300 pieces of artillery.

With the Swedes vanquished, what was Peter to do with such a brazen structure? Why, use it as a prison of course. The first inmate was Peter's own son, Tsarevich Alexey, who was not at all like his father and was suspected of even plotting against the towering monarch. (Although he relinquished his claim to the throne, Alexey was not spared the wrath of his father, who was not particularly good at handling dissidence. Unable to withstand tortuous lashings of the whip, Alexey also became the prison's first casualty.) Peter thus set a precedent that was followed by practically all his successors, including Lenin, who sent the mutinous Kronstadt sailors here in 1921 before shipping them off to Siberia or the firing squad. (Lenin might still have been sore about his older brother being interned here in 1887 along with others accused of plotting to assassinate Tsar Alexander III.) Other famous naughty boys forced to spend time here were Catherine the Great's critic Alexander Radishchev, the whole lot of relatively tame Decembrist rebels, and writers as diverse as Fyodor Dostoyevsky (whose death sentence was commuted as he awaited his turn in front of the firing squad), Maxim Gorky (who *faux-pased* by peddling revolutionary leaflets under a tsarist regime), and Nikolay Chernyshevsky (who made the most of his incarceration by writing his fittingly titled treatise *What is to be Done?*).

In predictable juxtaposition, the Peter and Paul Cathedral, a shrine to the Romanov dynasty, stands nearby the bastions within which its opponents wasted impotently away. Built in a Dutch style more reminiscent of Protestant traditions than of Orthodox ones (an idea of Peter, of course), the church's belfry supports the needlelike gilded spire that can be seen from all over the city. It was intended to be the highest structure in the country and to distinguish the St. Petersburg skyline from Moscow's. The church's interior, decorated in breathtaking Baroque and featuring a lovely carved iconostasis, houses the sarcophagi of the Romanov monarchs. (Nicholas II, who was finally given a proper burial here in 1998, was interned in a nearby chapel because he was buried along with some of his non-royal servants.) Peter the Great's tomb is easily discerned, being the only one topped by a bust of its occupant. Legend has it that Peter had his traitorous son Alexey buried beneath the aisle "so he would always be trampled on"; but don't believe every legend you hear.

Also of interest within the fortress is are a functioning mint, a boathouse, and a controversial statue of Peter the Great crafted by native sculptor Michael Shemyakin in 1991. Depicting the tsar as an aged, spindly pinhead, the delightful monument succeeds at serving up Soviet realism as well as historical distortion with a vengeance.

A cannon atop the Naryshkin Bastion (facing the Neva) traditionally is fired at noon, scaring the daylights out of tourists. On the other side of the bastion sunbathers in amusing, maximum-tan poses bake against the stone wall. If you get the tour group blues, seek out one of the fortress's makeshift outdoor cafés.

THE INSIDE SCOOP
As when in Moscow, the best bet for those wanting to tackle more than what is offered by shore excursions in St. Petersburg is to purchase a city-dedicated guidebook. For current

cultural and entertainment listings, consult the local English language newspapers *St. Petersburg Times* and *Neva News*. These publications as well as international ones can be found most easily inside one of the big hotels like Astoria, Grand Europe, or Nevsky Palace.

Because of high docking fees ships usually don't stay in St. Petersburg for much longer than two days. Such a brief visit to such an exciting city means two things: first, that organized shore excursions concentrate strictly on the main sights at a fairly brisk pace; second, that you might want to branch off on your own when you can to maximize your personal experience. Like in Moscow, the ship is moored some distance from the city center. You might want to consider avoiding any needless bus rides back to the ship (such as for lunch), as the process cuts into a sizable portion of the day. The shore excursions themselves are discussed briefly below.

Organized Shore Excursions

A "City Tour" is invariably conducted. It consists of a bus ride around the entire city with periodic stops at major sights for brief walks, picture-taking, and souvenir-buying. Although it's a bummer being carted around on a bus, this tour is probably the best way to get a comprehensive overview of St. Petersburg. The drawbacks to such a tour are that it can overwhelm, disorient, and certainly preclude any possibility of your not appearing like a rich Western tourist. Some city tours include a stop at St. Isaac's Cathedral. It's likely that you won't have time to give the cathedral the time it deserves, so if such a stop amounts to your only visit, you might have to abandon the tour here or come back on your own.

The "Hermitage Tour" provides the easiest access to and through the monstrous museum. Although it is entirely possible to visit the Hermitage on your own, the advantages of being with the tour group are that you skip the admission fee, you don't have to wait in long entrance lines, and you have your very own guide to impose a semblance of order on the madness that is the world's largest art collection.

The "Peter and Paul Fortress Tour" is simply a guided jaunt around the founding structural complex of St. Petersburg. If you cannot live without seeing the graves of Peter the Great and his descendants, then you better not miss this trip. If you can do without being shown around a historic prison with a pretty church, you might consider passing on this one. Souvenir vendors outside the main gate offer a good stock of Russian military memorabilia. Kiosks across the street sell pizzas, hot dogs, local draught beer, and other refreshments.

Half-day trips to one of St. Petersburg's country palaces always are offered. Whether the destination is Pushkin (Tsarskoye Selo), Peterhoff (Petrodvorets), or Pavlovsk, the trip is worthwhile, as these former monarchs' estates are filled with as much (if not more) history as any monument in the city center and surrounded by more beautiful landscaping than you'll see anywhere in Russia. Each is downright exquisite in its own way. The gardens and palace at Pushkin remind of Versailles; the gilded animated fountains of Peterhoff must be seen to be believed; and the "homey opulence" of Pavlovsk is charmingly unique. Of course if beholding royal extravagance isn't your cup of tea, you're infinitely better off not wasting a precious day away from the hard reality of the city.

Evening excursions typically comprise outings to the ballet. A disappointing pill to swallow is that the world-famous Mariinsky Theater (formerly the Kirov) is usually closed during summers while its first-string dance troupe is off dazzling foreign audiences. However, if your ship has arranged to visit the Hermitage Theater for an evening of ballet, you should not miss it, as the State Academic dancers hold their own, and the theater itself, a former private venue of the monarch, is exquisite and accessible only by special arrangement. Performances at other venues are usually put together for tour groups and tend to be respectable at best. The general problem is that most of the city's premier performing artists hit the road during the summer.

Other Possibilities

If you leave St. Petersburg without strolling its main lifeline, Nevsky Prospekt, you have failed to adequately tap into the pulse of the city. Here is where the nouveau riche rub elbows with the nouveau homeless, where Soviet *stolovayas* (greasy spoons) neighbor chic restaurants, where visitors from around the world haggle with street artists and souvenir peddlers. During a two-hour jaunt along Nevsky you can eat a Russian ice cream cone, buy a coffee table art book, pick up a fashionable pair of shoes, mail a letter, exchange currency, get a haircut, have your portrait painted, scarf down a hot dog, buy some Alka-Seltzer, and even make some new friends. Getting tired? Head to the beer garden hidden in a typical Petersburg courtyard directly across from the Nevsky Palace Hotel.

Another absolute must is a boat ride through the canals. Sure, it's something that only tourists do, but would you go to Venice without taking a spin in a gondola? Okay, it's not quite the same thing. But a canal ride is the most enjoyable way to glimpse parts of the city you would never otherwise see from a vantage-point you would never otherwise get. You can hire a boat where Nevsky Prospekt intersects either the Moika, Griboyedova, or Fontanka canals. The price is exorbitant, but why come all the way over here and deprive yourself of an unforgettable experience just to save the same amount of money you probably just threw away on a dumb fur hat? For the pinnacle of romance, grab a friend and a bottle of champagne and take a midnight ride, which can be especially magical during the white nights of June and July. You're sure to fall in love with the city, each other, or both.

For further cultural explorations check out exhibitions at the Russian Museum at Ploshchad Iskusstv (just off Nevsky Prospekt) and the Marble Palace at 5/1 Millionaya Ulitsa. For more leisurely wanderings try the famous Summer Garden, the setting for marathon drinking parties organized by Peter the Great, or the Alexander Nevsky Lavra, the burial site of tormented creative heroes such as Dostoyevsky, Tchaikovsky, and Musorgsky.

Past Dusk

For much of the summer, dusk in St. Petersburg never ends. Nonetheless your stomach still knows when it is dinner time, so you might want to sample a restaurant downtown rather than wearing your seat thin in the ship's dining hall. Listings in local publications can help point you in the right direction. You certainly cannot go wrong visiting any of the four dining establishments connected to the Grand Hotel Europe, right off Nevsky Prospekt. The Chopsticks (Chinese) and Rossi's (Italian/Continental) restaurants are truly first-rate, the formal Restaurant Europe serves five star gourmet delights, and the casual restaurant/bar Sadko's, featuring live music, is a meeting place for hipsters, expatriates, and businessmen. At 13 ulitsa Bolshaya Konyushennaya (off Nevsky Prospekt), a restaurant called Assembly offers swanky twenty-four hour dining, a traditional Russian menu, and a chance to rub elbows with the Petersburg underworld. Aphrodite, at Nevsky Prospekt 86, serves expensive but quality, Russian-style seafood.

For soaking up suds, English or German-style pubs include Chaika at 14 Canal Griboyedova, John Bull Pub at the bottom of Nevsky Prospekt, and the Beere Stube in the Nevsky Palace Hotel. Less expensive and funner places would be Mollie's Irish Pub, at 36 ulitsa Rubinshteina (metro Vladimirskaya), or the recently opened, much lauded Tinkoff Microbrewery, on Plekhanova behind Kazan Cathedral.

In terms of out-of-the-way local joints, it's difficult to find one that offers decent prices, palatable food, respectable service, and an acceptable atmosphere. Suggestions for non-Russian cuisine are Tandoor (2 Voznesensky Prospekt, near St. Isaac's Cathedral) for quality Indian dishes; Restaurant Le Français (20 Galernaya ulitsa) for pricey but authentic French cuisine; and newly opened Señor Pepe's Cantina for Mexican food at last done right. Anyone who is too tired to deal with the city and wants to feel really at home can call Pizza House (316-2666) for delivery right to the ship.

As elsewhere in Russia, nightlife in St. Petersburg revolves primarily around in-home entertaining. There are, however, a number of casinos, nightclubs, and discos that are more than willing to take your money. Hollywood Nights, on Nevsky Prospekt, with a restaurant, bar, casino, and nightclub, is probably the best bet for those wanted a quick taste of a Petersburg hotspot. Farther down Nevsky, Domenico's Nightclub/Restaurant is a slightly more intimate, but no less pricey alternative.

A final note. As they say in Mexico, don't drink the water. The suspicious liquid that flows out of St. Petersburg taps is definitely filled with undesirable metals, is purportedly plagued by a nasty parasite (giardia), and is possibly a bit radioactive.

WATERWAYS

Although the land distance between Moscow and St. Petersburg is only 650 kilometers, the river route between the two cities consists of ten separate bodies of water. (Technically the number is much greater if account is taken of the many various small reservoirs along the way.) Among the waterways traveled are Europe's largest lake, its longest river, and the world's longest man-made canal.

As you will learn, the Soviet government altered practically every waterway along the route in order to facilitate easier travel and gain sources of hydroelectricity. The Russian landscape is still majestic, and we have tried not to divert your attention from it too often. At times, though, it is difficult to refrain from informing about the rather reckless manner in which it was modified, especially when trying to provide straight answers to frequently asked questions like, "Why is the water so brown here?"

So much forest was flooded, so many species of fish pushed one step closer to extinction, and so many human lives displaced that it seemed irresponsible not to provide a little history about the formation of the present river network. As for the millions of political prisoners (most of whom were accomplished authors, professors, and scientists ordered to labor to the point of exhaustion by high school drop-out commanders) who perished while being forced to work on the undertakings—their plight merits remembrance.

The waterways are presented as they are encountered from Moscow to St. Petersburg.

Metric conversions useful for this chapter:

1 meter	= 1.09 yards (3.28 feet)
1 kilometer	= 0.62 miles
1 square kilometer	= 0.39 square miles
1 hectare	= 2.47 acres
1 cubic meter	= 1.30 cubic yards
1 cubic kilometer	= 0.24 cubic miles

MOSCOW CANAL

*A waterway from the Volga to Moscow is being made, which will
make inland Moscow a port!*
– *The Volga*, Soviet guidebook, 1932

Peter the Great dreamed of sailing unhindered from Moscow to St. Petersburg, a dream never fulfilled. Not until
1825 was the city of Moscow linked to the Volga—via a
canal to the Moscow River. This first canal was built
primarily to transport raw materials needed to build
Moscow's Church of Christ the Savior, an amazing architectural achievement later blown up by Stalin. Like the
church, the canal had a limited lifetime, eventually suffering
neglect due to the popularity of railroads.

Historically plagued by short water supply, Moscow by
the 1930s clearly needed to be linked to a major water
source. Well water utilized in the 1700s had long dried up;
spring water used in the 1800s had also been exhausted. A
1904 pipeline to the Moscow River provided relief for only
about twenty-five years, after which time the river had
become so depleted it could be crossed on foot in front of the
Kremlin.

In the 1930s, with Stalin championing a relentless surge
of technological advancement, no task was too grand for the
industry of socialism. Russia's historical heart and soul, the
Volga River, was targeted to solve Moscow's dilemma.
Two routes for a canal from Moscow to the Volga were
initially proposed. One followed existing streambeds and
older canal alleys. Its advantage was ease of building; its
disadvantage was its length (following the lay of the land, it
tended to wind a bit). The other proposal more or less
followed the bed of the Yakhroma River, joining the Volga
west of the present town of Dubna. Both proposals ultimately were rejected in favor of the present day canal, which

bullies its way straight to the Volga in true Stalinist fashion.

Also true to Stalinist fashion, the endeavor was carried out with great haste and with absolute disregard for the lives of the GULAG prisoners who were forced to dig it out shovelful by shovelful. Like many enterprises undertaken during this dubious period of Soviet technological expansion, the canal was built for subjects of the regime on the bones of subjects of the regime.

The feat, however, was undeniably awesome. The entire project required building 240 "complicated constructions," including 7 concrete dams, 8 earthen dams, 11 locks, 8 hydroelectric plants, 5 pump stations, 15 bridges, 2 tunnels, and the Northern River Passenger Terminal with its accompanying cargo port. During the 5 years of the canal's construction, workers excavated over 200 million cubic meters of earth and poured over 3 million cubic meters of concrete along its 128 kilometer length. The scope of the task surpassed that of either the Panama or Suez canals.

On 15 July 1937 inland Moscow woke up as a port connected by water to all of Russia's five major seas. The capital also gained a source of hydroelectricity as well as a new stretch of recreational areas.

Ship navigators appreciate the canal's reliable depth, straight course, and wind-sheltered aspect. Passengers tend to enjoy the canal's placidity, its occasionally high-banked surroundings, and vistas of countryside afforded by its elevated bed.

Engineering buffs might be interested to note some of the canal's special features, including round "emergency towers" protruding from the canal walls at various intervals. From these towers cables are able to raise an underwater concrete gate. These "cut-off gates" can dam up a section of canal which can then be drained by a floating pump station in order to perform maintenance, inspection, etc. Also of interest is that between Lock # 2 and the reservoirs beyond Lock # 6 the Volga waters are actually pumped through the canal.

Total time of passage from the Northern River Terminal to the Volga junction: approximately ten hours.

VOLGA RIVER

The Volga is Russia herself—her people, her history, her nature.
– Markov Yevgeniy, early century Russian writer

The Volga of the towpath is gone, replaced by a new, socialist Volga.
– People's Commissariat for Waterway Transit, 1932

It is time to stop the degradation of the Volga. Today is not too late. Tomorrow it is hardly possible.
– Social Committee to Save the Volga, 1989

From its remote source in the Valdai Hills northwest of Moscow, the Volga River meanders up to the Rybinsk Reservoir, changes direction, commences winding southeast to Kazan before twisting westward to Volgograd where it plunges finally southward to the Caspian Sea. Its 3,688 kilometer length makes it the longest river in Europe.

The rivership journey explores only a fraction of its snaking course, thus bypassing much of what is referred to as the "Volga region," the heartland of Russia. Ships not traveling to Yaroslavl and Kostroma sail only 220 kilometers of the river (from the Moscow Canal to the Rybinsk Reservoir), while those making the side trip cover about 200 additional kilometers of upper Volga. Both these stretches, however, comprise what chartmen call the "real Russian Volga," a region close to the river's source and endowed with as many quaint villages and neat plots of farmland as it is with colorful legends and tales.

The Volga is Russia's principal waterway, connected via a network of man-made canals to all five of the country's major seas. Half of all river freight in Russia is transported on its waters, which are also used to irrigate the steppes of the South. The river usually is navigable from March to mid-December. Early summer months can bring flooding, while in the later part of the summer, low water levels expose shoals and sandbars.

The Greek philosopher Ptolemy first mentioned the Volga in the 2nd century, comparing its grandeur to that of the Nile. By the 8th century Slavs were relying on the river as a trade route to the Middle East. During the flourishing of Kievan Rus in the 11th and 12th centuries, merchant settlements sprung up along the Volga's banks, and neighboring lands were cultivated. When Ivan the Terrible conquered Kazan and Astrakhan in the 16th century, the entire length of the river finally became the domain of the united Russian lands. (Since that time the Russians have rightly believed that with the Volga intact the country is never conquered.) In the early 19th century the first Volga steamships appeared.

In the 20th century the river was chopped into a chain of vast reservoirs in the socialist quest to supply the country with hydroelectricity. Although the hydroelectric station at Rybinsk was integral to the survival of Moscow during World War II, most scientists today agree that the damming of the Volga turned out to be a colossal ecological as well as economic mistake. Not only was the filling of reservoirs carried out irresponsibly—forming large basins of flooded forests which destroy the ecosystem—but the flooding of valuable plowland ended up costing Russia much more than what it gained in hydroelectricity. Scientists also concede that the flagrant disregard shown to the thousands of Russian people who inhabited the Volga valleys before those valleys became reservoirs is not something to be particularly proud of either.

Your journey luckily misses the big Volga reservoirs (with the notable exception of the Rybinsk Reservoir). The stretches it does cover, perhaps somewhat more swollen than in the past, constitute parts of the river that still flow in their mischievous natural beds. A lone Volga fisherman in his rowboat in the soft twilight of dusk or sporadic campfires glowing amidst forested embankments in the dark of morning still reveal the majesty of the famed waterway that "flows in the heart of every Russian," *Matushka Volga*, "Dear Mother Volga."

RYBINSK RESERVOIR

A man should have a sense of responsibility for all that people do,
and for the way they live.
– Lev Tolstoy

Before the formation of the Rybinsk Reservoir, great rivers such as Volga, Sheksna, and Mologa joined in a mire of ever-changing junctions, tributaries, and rivulets on a vast plain settled by lively merchant communities. Here pumped the vital mercantile artery between the Russian North and South, connecting the rich northern forests with the fertile southern plains of the Volga and Don. There was a problem, though. The artery's blood tended to run thin during summer, the peak navigational period. Rivers, especially the Volga, dried so much they could be crossed without raising the leg of one's trousers. The locks of the Mariinskaya System were ill-equipped to solve the problem, as their capacity was limited by their size as well as by the shallow stretches between them. Often pulled from one lock to another with ropes, ships took up to three months to travel between Rybinsk and St. Petersburg.

Enter Josef Stalin and the "Big Volga" plan of 1932. Voting on an ambitious proposal to dam the Volga and Sheksna in order to create a massive reservoir, Stalin pronounced, "I am for it!" Thus the fate of 700 villages that would be flooded by the reservoir's construction was sealed. Documents reveal that, in true Stalinist fashion, "alternatives were not discussed." From the beginning the project was classified; the general public was not told of its blatant recklessness.

By 1936, when construction of the reservoir was in full swing, control of the project was turned over to Stalin's notorious Committee of Internal Affairs, which administrated the forced labor of GULAG prisoners. A "worker" recalls the job site:

There were chains of guards everywhere. They
watched all the prisoners, most of whom were
charged with Article 58 (political dissent).
They were very educated people. Maybe that's
why they died the quickest—because it was
more difficult for them to bear the unfairness
of it. The food was awful. About 100 people
died per day.

Yes, the construction of the reservoir put an end to tsarist
methods of transport, ensuring that never again would
"weary men toil along the endless towpath, straining at the
rope by which they hauled their masters' heavy-laden
barges." But it did so by filling mass graves with the
grandsons of those weary men.

The filling of the reservoir began in 1941. As village
families collected their belongings and began walking to
unknown destinations, the flooding of over 4,000 hectares
of fertile plowland commenced. After the water's initial
brown murkiness settled, it eventually took on a greenish
hue due to floating "seaweed." This seaweed, visible today,
is actually the decay of submerged forests and depletes the
water of its natural oxygen content. Rybinsk Reservoir,
whose name derives from the word *ryba*, or "fish," becomes
a larger and larger fish cemetery each year.

More than 60 rivers join the reservoir, which occupies an
area of 4,500 square kilometers. Its vast size, not its average
depth of only five meters, often earns it the name of Rybinsk
Sea. The water can be turbulent at times, but don't worry,
buoys along the way constantly broadcast weather conditions to ships' radios. Ships not diverting down the Volga
to Yaroslavl and Kostroma cross the full length of the
reservoir on a north-south axis. Those making the side trip
likewise navigate the full length, but pass through the
Rybinsk Hydroplant on the southeastern reach, thus entering and exiting the reservoir twice.

VOLGA-BALTIC CANAL

"We shall have whatever we need."
– Tsar Peter the Great

THE PAST: MARIINSKAYA SYSTEM

Between the southern reach of Lake Onega and the northern end of the Rybinsk Reservoir the ship navigates the Volga-Baltic Canal, opened in 1964. Prior to this time ships traveling between the two bodies of water were obliged to navigate the locks and canals of the Mariinskaya System, a man-made waterway originally undertaken by order of Peter the Great. Peter dearly wanted to include in the project the junction of the Vytegra and Kovzha rivers—a union vital to the canal's continuity—but never was able to realize the goal. Not until 1810, when the Mariinskaya System was expanded, were those rivers, as well as other parts of the route covered by the present day canal, at last linked. The system was augmented and upgraded several times during the 19th century, yet its desired efficiency was always evasive. In the 1930s the Soviet government decided to completely overhaul the Mariinskaya System. Although several phases of the project were finished by 1940, most of the work was interrupted by World War II. Finally, in 1964, the Volga-Baltic Canal fully replaced the Mariinskaya System as the country's principal canal network. Several segments of the old system, such as canals around Lake Ladoga, Lake Onega, and the White Lake, still operate, although their usage is minimal. Several of the thirty-nine old wooden locks can still be seen while sailing between St. Petersburg and the Volga.

THE PRESENT: VOLGA-BALTIC CANAL

The Volga-Baltic Canal is probably the most confusing part of the journey between Moscow and St. Petersburg because it is composed of several prominent and distinct bodies of water. They are (from south to north) the **Sheksna River**, the **White Lake**, the **Kovzha River**, the **Water Division Canal**, and the **Vytegra Canal**.

The Soviets, being fond of such proclamations, liked to call the 360 kilometer-long canal the longest in the world, even though its length does not entirely constitute man-made waterways. In fact the canal is comprised mostly of natural river and lake beds. However by damming the constituent rivers and erecting hydroplants, the Soviets certainly altered existing routes by carelessly flooding them. So in the final analysis, perhaps the thing is man made after all. Whatever it is, it comprises eight locks, nearly as many hydroelectric stations, as well as numerous dams, reservoirs, and bridges. A significant if not somewhat unintelligible feature of the canal is that it connects the slopes of what are known as the Baltic Sea and Caspian Sea water basins. Upon completion, the canal, naturally, was named after Lenin.

The landscape of the Volga-Baltic Canal region is alternately enchanting and graceless. At times the canal narrows to such an extent that thick foliage on the banks practically brushes the hull of the ship; at other times the banks disappear altogether into murky expanses of flooded forest. Some stretches present quaint villages of carved cottages adjacent to fields of rye, oat, barley, or flax, while in other places industrialized towns confront the river with gray jungles of mills and machinery. Dense deciduous and coniferous forests endow the region with a dark majesty, but also provide it with economic sustenance by disappearing at the spinning teeth of roaring chain saws. Timber yards, wood freighters, storehouses, and mills are noticeable all along the canal's length. At last check, forests still occupied two-thirds of the region, but it is uncertain how long that figure will hold.

Wildlife that might be spotted amidst the trees include such sizable creatures as moose and elk. In the water swim pike, perch, bream, and burbot.

Sheksna River (186 kilometers)

Connecting the Rybinsk Reservoir to the White Lake, the Sheksna River is composed of three segments: the Upper Sheksna (52 kilometers), the Sheksna Reservoir (66 kilometers), and the Lower Sheksna (68 kilometers). The former two segments are separated from the latter by a dam at the Sheksna Hydroplant and are often together referred to as the Sheksna Reservoir. The name Sheksna is thought to be derived from a Finnish term meaning "a sedge-covered tributary." (Sedge, by the way, is a grass-like plant found in swamps and on riverbanks.) Ever since the times of Kievan Rus, when brave men-at-arms would battle its rapids, this sedge-lined tributary has played a vital role by connecting the northern lands to the Volga.

The original construction of the Mariinskaya System left the Sheksna completely intact. Subsequent upgrading called for straightening the riverbed and incorporating a network of locks. The Volga-Baltic Canal demanded more alterations, such as substantial widening and deepening of parts as well as the implementation of a hydroplant. Vast areas of forest were flooded and now make up much of the riverside landscape, especially along the reservoir proper.

White Lake

Mention of the ancient White Lake has been frequent in Russian history and folklore ever since its shores were settled by Veps tribes in the 8th century. Ever since, it has served as trade bridge between Russia's North and South. In the 17th century the lake became known as the "tsar's fishing grounds" because government boats cruised around enforcing a fish tax on all fishermen but those from nearby monasteries. (Tsars knew that taxing God was a no-no.)

The lake was incorporated into the Mariinskaya System in the 19th century and subsequently into the Volga-Baltic Canal. Like the canal's natural rivers, the lake did not escape manipulation. It was used to absorb the overflow of the Sheksna River, a role that influenced its natural currents and flooded portions of its shores. The circular shoreline, formed over a period of thousands of years, suddenly disappeared, and decaying, submerged forests soon endangered the underwater ecosystem. An ecological station was recently set up in the lakeside city of Belozersk to monitor the lake and "cure the wounds" inflicted on it by the Volga-Baltic Canal's construction.

A host of rivers flows into the White Lake, contributing to its 1,400 square kilometer area. Only one river, the Sheksna, drains the lake. (With its damming, however, the Sheksna can clog the lake as well.) The lake bottom, for the most part, is uniformly flat and sandy, making for a consistent depth of five meters. Northern winds occasionally induce sizable daytime swells, while fogs can creep in and cover the lake during still nights. For most of the summer, though, ships count on smooth and easy sailing.

Kovzha River (43 kilometers)

Between the Water Division Canal and the northern end of the White Lake the Kovzha River runs more or less in its historical bed. In formerly winding places the river's course has been redirected some, but spots like the Konstantinovskiye Rapids, at the northern end of the river, still retain their shallow and rocky formidableness. Because so many other rivers and streams feed into the Kovzha, damming caused its banks to overrun extensively. Nevertheless its wide areas of flooded forest as well as its occasional tree-lined narrow necks lend the Kovzha landscape a sense of remote if not somewhat wistful splendor.

Water Division Canal (53 kilometers)

Certainly better than what Peter the Great had in mind, this narrow canal, dug in 1963, at last joined the Vytegra and Kovzha rivers without the use of locks. Peter, of course, did not have access to the dredges and excavators the Soviets used to push around over 31 million cubic meters of earth. The reason for the canal's name is that it officially marks the joining of Russia's sheer northern slope with its sloping southern one, forming a plateau of sorts between the Baltic and Caspian water basins.

Vytegra Canal (38 kilometers)

This segment consists of a thirteen kilometer-long canal, beginning at the southern end of Lake Onega, and three subsequent reservoirs. The canal portion, being narrow and shallow, requires navigators' close attention. Because of its frequent usage and clay bottom, its water often is a dark brown cast. The Vytegra region is known for its substantial timber output, which includes an unusually resonant variety of fir used for crafting musical instruments. Also it was here on a forested hillside (now an island in one of the reservoirs) that Peter the Great spent ten days consulting with engineers and scratching his head over the dilemma of connecting the Vytegra and Kovzha rivers.

LAKE ONEGA

With a shape resembling that of a one-clawed lobster, Lake Onega spans a 10,000 square kilometer area, making it the second largest lake in Europe, bowing in size only to its twice-larger neighbor, Lake Ladoga. Depths of the lake average 30 meters, but include cavities reaching as far down as 120 meters. More than 50 rivers and 1,000 streams feed Onega, but only the Svir River, which connects it to Ladoga, originates from Onega. The lake contains over 1,300 islands, most of which lie in the north where forests of pine stand at the edges of rocky, jagged coastline. Linden and elm trees are more common in the middle and southern areas, where sandy shores slope into shallow bays of reeds.

Primitive tribes from as early as the first century are among the hardy settlers who historically have inhabited the shores of Lake Onega. (Petroglyphs found on the cliffs of its eastern shores are on view in St. Petersburg's Hermitage Museum.) The abundance of natural beauty as well as wildlife doubtlessly contributed to the appeal of the Onega region. The lake sustains more than forty species of fish, including formidable freshwater salmon and trout. (The trout population actually was started artificially with fish from Lake Sevan in Armenia.) Bays are home to some 200 varieties of birds, including ducks, swans, cranes, and geese. Prowling through the surrounding forests are bears, elks, foxes, wolves, hares, and squirrels. Doing more paddling than prowling, muskrats are also prominent; how they got here from North America no one knows.

The water itself is quite a lure, as its purity is practically unsurpassable. Although of a dark shade, it boasts a mineral composition second in purity only to distilled water. With such a strong natural attribute, the lake has thus far been able to resist the polluting tendencies of humankind.

The lake's location in the rugged northern republic of Karelia makes for a severe climate. Air temperatures dip below freezing for half of the year, and frequent storms can generate swells as high as five meters on the lake surface. Onega's renowned misty dawns of June and autumnal symphonies of shoreline colors, however, never cease amazing thousands of annual visitors, many of whom come to behold the miraculous wooden churches on Kizhi Island.

SVIR RIVER

The water of the River Svir mirrors
the sunlit sky of midnight,
gulls sully by in pairs,
and Anton, a crew-boy, teaches
words for everything beheld.

The water of the River Svir reveals
a debt to ancestors who seeded
blood with eerie draw
to this severe wonderland.

– an enchanted river traveler

The Svir River stretches 215 kilometers through northern forests below Karelia, connecting Europe's two largest lakes, Ladoga, to the west, and Onega, to the east. The Svir landscape, rugged and majestic, cannot help but entrance the shipboard observer. At times the banks take on the form of reddish, forested precipices; at others they slope smoothly into green marshes.

Ever since the first settlements appeared along the river over 5,000 years ago the region has been considered severe and wild. Even during the 13th century, when the river belonged to Novgorod and Mongol-Tatar domination caused people to flee the cities, few settlers dared to strike into the area's impenetrable forests and foggy marshlands. During tsarist times the Svir region was a place of exile; during the communist era it was targeted for hydropower potential.

Regardless of the country's political situation, the Svir and its forests have always provided Russia with timber. Even today the main occupation of those living along the Svir is lumbering. Log piles, timber rafts, and storage sheds can be seen all along the river's expanse, including the reaches of its thirty tributaries. Pine and fir continue to line the shores without interruption, though, as they help to preserve the banks and regulate the water level.

The river's depth reaches five meters in autumn and closer to ten meters in spring. (The water level is actually regulated by the "needs" of the river's two hydroplants.) The river usually freezes from December to April, but during warmer winters it may not totally solidify. From the water local fishermen reel in salmon and trout in addition to smaller pan fish. The quality of the water, however, is anybody's guess. In hazarding a guess, don't necessarily let the river's browness influence you—the coloring can be attributed to the flooding of the banks necessitated and maintained by the Svir's two hydroplants.

Somewhat of a nightmare from a navigational standpoint, the Svir is plagued by shallow stretches, narrow rapids, blind bends, dense fogs, and the constant threat of floating debris such as tree trunks and coagulations of peat. During the first half of this century river captains relied on wooden navigational buoys to aid their course; the buoys were not entirely reliable, however, as the kerosene lamps within had to be lit by hand from a rowboat. Today all 1,070 modern buoys are lit automatically. So sit back, relax, and drink in the spectacle of soft northern night caressing one of the voyage's most serene waterways.

LAKE LADOGA

Covering an area of 18,000 square kilometers and containing 900 cubic kilometers of water, Lake Ladoga resembles a sea more than a landlocked body of freshwater. Known for a moody temperament and surrounded by austere beauty, Europe's largest lake can challenge the nautical sense of a river captain as well as the visual sense of a first-time visitor.

The lake is characterized by extremes. Depths in its northern parts reach as far down as 230 meters, while in the south, stony, shallow areas can impede navigation. The landscape of its rugged northern shores comprises sheer, jagged precipices and sharply cut bays; these features likewise define the north's 500 remote islands and skerries. By contrast, southern shores constitute sloping, sandy beaches on both sides of the lake's 130 kilometer width. More than 30 rivers supply Ladoga with water; yet only one river, the Neva, flows from it. The water warms slowly in summer and freezes equally slowly in winter.

Baltic salmon and Baltic sturgeon are among the numerous species of fish inhabiting Lake Ladoga. One of the more anomalous species of the lake's water-going wildlife is the Ladoga seal, an ancient creature which migrated from the White Sea.

Historically Ladoga has not only supported a diverse northern ecosystem, but also the inhabitants of its closest metropolis, St. Petersburg. Called Leningrad during World War II, the former capital was designated a "hero city" of the Soviet Union for persevering through the harrowing German blockade of 1941-44. For its vital role in aiding the city during the ungodly siege, Lake Ladoga might be considered a "hero lake." Although the deaths of over one million Leningraders were not averted, food rations and other supplies essential to the city's survival were transported across the lake. Further casualties were avoided by evacuating nearly one million citizens over lake routes. In summers boats braved Luftwaffe bombs, while during some of the most frigid winters of the century trucks drove as far as 110 kilometers across the ice on what was called Ladoga's "Road of Life."

Today the lake continues to sustain St. Petersburg by supplying the city with its main source of drinking water. Unfortunately this role is less heroic than that of the past, as the lake is close to biological death due to phosphate pollution caused most prominently by the lakeside industrial town of Priozersk. More alarming, in 1990 divers discovered a shipwreck that had lain on the lake bed for thirty years leaking (gulp) radioactivity.

The only threat Lake Ladoga poses to the visiting rivership passenger, however, is rough water in late summer. During the eight-hour trip to Valaam Island in the northeast of the lake, it is possible to encounter swells of three to six meters. Although riverships are fairly accurately described as acting like "a small cart on a stone-paved road," none have gone down in recent memory. In fact Dramamine addicts may rest assured that for the better part of the summer the voyage across the immense body of water is perfectly tranquil and, frankly, totally uneventful.

16.

17.

18.

19.

NEVA RIVER

Deriving its source from Lake Ladoga, the Neva runs for a total of 74 kilometers to the Finnish Bay of the Baltic Sea, where it fans out into a 280 square kilometer basin. The name of the river is derived from the Finnish word *nevo*, for "marshy," which is an adequate description of its massive estuary. First claimed for Russia by the Novgorod principality in the 9th century, the Neva was always a bone of contention between the Swedes and Russians. Peter the Great finally consolidated Russia's claim to the river with his victory over Sweden in the Northern War of 1700-21. To show his intention of holding onto the river, he founded his new capital, St. Petersburg, at its mouth.

Indeed the Neva is an integral part of St. Petersburg, which spreads atop forty-two of the river's islands and is divided by a system of river-fed canals. Although such an aspect creates an effect reminiscent of Venice or Amsterdam, historically it has meant lots of flooding. While walking around St. Petersburg you might occasionally spy a plaque showing the water level in the city during some of the more devastating floods, such as those of 1824 and 1924. The Neva, along with Lake Ladoga, also supplies St. Petersburg with drinking water. "Drinking water," however, is a bit of a misnomer, as the Neva, like other great rivers that have been destined to pass through major cities, is fairly well polluted.

The voyage by rivership between St. Petersburg and Lake Ladoga is quite scenic, as the Neva boasts some dramatically high banks (between 6 and 9 meters) and a width varying from 250 to 1,300 meters. Within twenty-five kilometers of the St. Petersburg city limit the river landscape comprises suburbs and villages. More natural settings are encountered farther from the city. Depths along the way range from eight to twenty-four meters. The current moves at an average speed of four kilometers per hour, except at a bottlenecked section called the Ivanovskiye Rapids, where the pace quickens. Due to the river's proximity to the Baltic Sea, its surrounding climate tends to be rather damp and rainy. Even during the peak summer month of July the temperature on the water rarely reaches above 25° centigrade (78° Fahrenheit).

TOPICS OF INTEREST

To enhance your enjoyment and understanding of the sights you will be touring and the information you will be assimilating, we have dared to summarize major topics like Russian history, architecture, and religion. We have also put together some advice to help you become the knowledgeable souvenir shopper you know you want to be. Presenting a ruble exchange rate here would be laughable, as the value of Russian currency changes faster than you can say perestroika.

We will say a word about the Russian calendar, however, as it may effect your understanding of significant dates. In 1700 Peter the Great finally replaced Russia's old Byzantine calendar with the Julian calendar, a more effective version used in Western Europe since 1582. Peter's timing was bad, though, for shortly after his decree Europe changed to the even more effective Gregorian calendar (the one in use today). Russia didn't follow suit as usual, and by the 20th century it found itself lagging a full two weeks behind the rest of the world. The Soviets finally straightened the matter out by adopting the Gregorian calendar in 1918. That year January 31 was decreed to be February 14. This discrepancy explains why the Soviets celebrated the October Revolution in November. Because Orthodox holidays are still based on the Julian calendar, Russians to this day celebrate Christmas on January 7.

In this book, we have dated events by the calendar officially in use in Russia at the time. In other words, the Julian calendar is used before 1918 and the Gregorian thereafter. This method of documenting Russian history is the most common, so don't feel you've been cheated out of two weeks like those poor folks in 1918.

RUSSIAN ARCHITECTURE

While visiting Moscow, St. Petersburg, and the provinces between them, you encounter architectural styles ranging from Byzantine to Medieval to Old Russian to Baroque to Neo-Classical to Art Nouveau. That's great, but what does it all mean?

Church Architecture

Because the Russian Orthodox Church descends from Constantinople, church architecture in Russia has its roots in Byzantine traditions. The Chronicles state that Russian ambassadors to Constantinople were so taken by that city's churches that they reported, "We did not know if we were in heaven or on earth... we only knew that there, God is present among men." Accordingly, the first church structures in Kiev (the first center of the Russian Church) emulated Constantinople's.

Although Russian churches evolved on their own, their initial layout remained faithful to that of mid-Byzantine churches. The design is called *cross-in-square*, which in simplest terms means that the building is essentially square, divided by the shape of a broad cross into nine *bays*, or sections, including the large center bay which forms the church's *nave*, or main interior space. The central bay is crowned by a large dome. Smaller domes often are situated over the four corner bays.

These conventional domes eventually gave rise to the ubiquitous Russian-style cupola, or "onion dome." As cultural, religious, and political activities moved from Kiev to the northern regions of Novgorod, Vladimir, and Pskov, the domes became more pointed, most likely to facilitate snow runoff. These "helmet domes" became separated from the roof itself by windowed cylinders called *drums*. In order to keep out the cold, the windows on the drums grew steadily narrower as the drums themselves grew longer. By and by the cupolas themselves stretched increasingly heavenward, and the bulbous "onion dome" was born.

Also at this time (roughly 12th-13th century) the genesis of another distinctly Russian architectural element, called the *kokoshnik* gable, was taking place. Curved gable-ends were incorporated below the roof's central drum, which created the effect of a stepped pyramid starting at the roofline and terminating at the top of the cupola. These arch-like gable-ends gradually became slightly pointed, perhaps to mimic the shape of the cupola itself, but not to imitate the Gothic arch, as is often falsely assumed. This element reached maturity once the political tide shifted to Moscow, where the decorative arches were arranged in ascending tiers, forming the uniquely Russian *kokoshniky* which lead the eye dramatically and elegantly upward to the cupola. The Annunciation Cathedral in the Moscow Kremlin is one of many churches you will see that make splendid use of *kokoshnik* gables.

The cross-in-square layouts eventually were augmented with adjoining chapels, exterior galleries, porches, and often a tent-shaped belfry. These additions, in combination with the elements mentioned above, came to form what is commonly referred to as traditional Russian church architecture. Attention-grabbing St. Basil's Cathedral on Red Square, often considered to embody the traditional Russian style, was at the time of its construction actually an unparalleled departure from convention. Essentially a "tent-shaped" church (i.e., spire-like rather than utilizing drums and domes) amidst a conglomeration of distinct chapels, St. Basil's represented an eclectic and unprecedented mix of elements priorly seen only on wooden churches.

Secular Architecture

Peter the Great altered the course of Russian architecture by forbidding building in stone anywhere but his new city of St. Petersburg, where only Western-style structures were allowed. This shift away from concentrating on church architecture in favor of secular structures spelled the beginning of the Baroque in Russia. The initial Petrine Baroque was rather restrained in that it remained based on north-European prototypes rather than on Western Baroque structures with their exuberant decoration, curvaceous forms, and complex spatial arrangements. Good examples of Petrine Baroque in St. Petersburg are Peter's yellow Summer Palace in the Summer Garden as well as Menshikov's Palace and the red brick St. Petersburg University building, both on the Neva embankment.

Under Empress Elizabeth (1741-61), Russian Baroque reached its peak. Directed by Russian as well as European architects—most notably Italian Bartolomeo Rastrelli—the city's building projects, including the grandiose Winter Palace and the palace at Peterhoff, became more truly Baroque. St. Petersburg's Smolny Cathedral, started by Rastrelli, is an intriguing example of this period in that it incorporates traditional Russian onion domes into a dominant Baroque design. Had Rastrelli finished the cathedral, examples of Rococo motifs would have been added. As it turned out, Elizabeth eventually ran out of funds, so true Rococo features never really made it into Russia.

Elizabeth's bankruptcy brought the Baroque period in Russia to an abrupt halt. Catherine the Great (1762-96) championed Russia's next sweeping architectural phase, called Neo-Classicism. The empress commissioned large-scale buildings in both the capital and provinces. These structures were designed as a reaction against the frippery of Late Baroque and favored a more simple approach to building, as attained by the Classicism of the early Greeks. The dominant belief was that society as well as architecture are at their best in their purest forms. Thus a return to the Classical orders and to strict geometric shapes was exhibited in new buildings throughout the country.

Although true Classical purity of either society or architecture was never really regained, Neo-Classical architecture dominated many Russian cities such as Kostroma, Yaroslavl, and most prominently, St. Petersburg. The latter became one of the most consistently Neo-Classical cities of Europe; its colored stucco facades with details picked out in white still create a sense of grandiose theatricality.

Russia's attention turned back to Moscow after the 1917 Revolution. Although interesting Art Nouveau work was demonstrated there on such buildings as the Metropol Hotel, the city was soon ruthlessly remodeled to reflect the "triumphant march of socialism" spearheaded by Stalin. Buildings returned to a reliance on heavy Classical motifs. Streets were bulldozed and widened to create huge boulevards and squares fit for grand proletarian pageants. The result, however, was an imposing, inhuman environment.

Among the most bizarre architectural styles to be seen in Russia is that dubbed "Stalinist Gothic," exhibited chiefly by seven ominous skyscrapers planted about Moscow. The Northern River Terminal, with its towering, red star-capped spire is also representative of this "Gotham City" look.

Unimaginative reconstruction plagued many Russian cities besides Moscow after the damage inflicted on them by World War II. With ecclesiastical architecture abolished and civic structures executed in an uninspired fashion dictated primarily by modern construction methods, the last notable albeit dubious contribution to Russian architecture was the mercilessly drab, prefabricated blocks of concrete that provided cramped residential space to Soviet citizens. Dubbed *khrushchevky* after the Party leader whose term in office saw their completion, these ill-constructed and often unfinished apartment complexes had the effect of blighting city landscapes and making Soviet citizens pine for the integrity of earlier Neo-Classical structures or even the spaciousness of Stalin-period architecture.

ORTHODOX RELIGION

The best way to avoid the doldrums sometimes caused by visiting so many Orthodox churches and monasteries is to arm yourself with a little knowledge about the religion itself. Here is a brief overview of the Church's evolution to let you know what all the fuss is about.

Notwithstanding a seventy year hiatus during Soviet times, the practices of Eastern Orthodoxy have defined Russian spirituality and pervaded Russian social, cultural, and political life since the 10th century. The Russian Orthodox Church is the largest single branch of the Eastern Orthodox religion, which numbers over 125 million followers and spans primarily across Eastern Europe as well as parts of the Middle East.

Prior to the 10th century Slavs and other tribes inhabiting present-day Russia and Ukraine carried on pagan traditions, oriented around respect for and harmony with the forces of nature. Their rituals included presenting eggs, honey, and wheat to various gods representing the water, sun, and soil. Families elaborately decorated their homes with carved figures of mermaids, suns, and other divine symbols. The unifying belief in this system was that everything in the universe is interconnected and that humankind must not impose its will on natural phenomena but rather unobtrusively take its place among a natural order that functions according to powers much greater than human will. Pagan beliefs not only united communities, but enabled ancient agricultural peoples to befriend nature, to learn from and thrive on the world around them.

It was the idea of Grand Prince Vladimir I (980-1015) to introduce monotheism to Kievan Rus as part of his efforts to unify a growing domain divided by clans and self-contained communities. According to legend, Vladimir, not knowing which monotheism was best, "tried on" the tenets of various religions to see how they suited his personal taste and political aims. He pondered Judaism but thought it too geographically scattered; he summarily dismissed the Muslim faith—even though it allowed harems—because it forbade alcohol; and he found Roman Christianity unappealing because the Pope claimed political precedence over secular princes such as himself. In the end the matter was settled when Vladimir married the sister of the Byzantine Emperor, thus becoming aligned with Eastern Christianity, which had developed in Constantinople independently from Rome ever since 330 A.D.

Vladimir persuaded the patriarch of Constantinople to send envoys to open up shop in Kiev in 988, thus marking the founding of the Russian Orthodox Church. The religion brought with it Byzantine influences in culture, art, and architecture which were to contribute to the formation of the Russian identity for the next one thousand years.

In 1300 the seat of the Russian Church moved from Kiev to Vladimir. Twenty years later it moved to Moscow where it still is located today. Although no central governing body presides over the Church, the holy patriarch of Russia (Alexiy II at present) is its highest official. A council called the Holy Synod helps in the administration department. The patriarch lives at the Church's headquarters in the St. Daniil Monastery in Moscow, although Church business is now being increasingly conducted at the Trinity Monastery of St. Sergius (formerly Zagorsk), just outside of Moscow.

Perhaps never before in history has Christianity been so boldly and so summarily suppressed than during Soviet rule in Russia. Accusing the Church of being as ideologically oppressive as the monarchy as well as fundamentally antithetical to communist ideology (not to mention being a capitalist enterprise), the Bolsheviks in 1917 closed all churches and instituted prohibition on religion. Over the next several decades more than 90,000 churches were either blown up or ruinously neglected. Of those 7,000 or so that remained standing, many were put to secular use, housing workshops, storage units, or swimming pools.* Particularly significant monasteries and churches were converted into "museums of national cultural history."

In 1988 the Orthodox Church celebrated its millennium by retaining its legal status in Russia. Since then the government has been steadily returning to the Church all structures confiscated by the Soviets. It hasn't been a particularly well-organized process, often resulting in disputes between buildings' secular tenants and their reinstated Orthodox proprietors. Religious services, however, have commenced once again throughout the country. Over 50 million Russian, Byelorussian, and Ukrainian citizens have officially rejoined the Church. Parents once again baptize their babies and take their children to Sunday schools.

A visit to Russia is not complete without observing an Orthodox service. The ethereal singing of the choir, the solemn presence of candles, the mystical odor of incense, and the bearded, black-robed priests scattering holy water on the devout create an atmosphere as revealing of religious tradition as of national history. Even during inactive hours gatherings of faithful stand before the iconostasis bowing and crossing themselves incessantly as *babushkas* bustle about sweeping and polishing the floor. Inside the churches pews and statues are absent, while frescoes and icons abound. The exit is always to the west and always beneath a rendering of the Last Judgment—a guilt trip to go, if you will. Women are expected to cover their heads while inside, men to uncover theirs. Photography is usually permitted upon paying a small fee.

* For a look at a church nave converted into a swimming pool (now in the process of being restored to a place of worship), visit St. Peter's Lutheran Church at 22-24 Nevsky Prospekt in St. Petersburg.

RUSSIAN LEADERS

While touring Russia you are sure to hear the names of its various leaders thrown around in connection with events, foundings, and historical periods. Indeed everything composing Russian history seems to be inextricably connected to its rulers, as autocracy and dictatorship have determined the direction of the country throughout its existence. To help clarify the historical information you'll receive along the way, a comprehensive chronology of rulers is here provided.

Rurik of Novgorod (862-79) – Norseman who founded Novgorod, thus giving birth to the Russian state and the Rurik dynasty.

Oleg of Kiev (879-912) – Moved the capital from Novgorod to Kiev, setting the stage for city rivalry that divided the country until 1478.

Igor (912-46) – Exacted heavy taxes on Slavs, who tied him to two trees and ripped him in half.

Olga (946-69) – Widow of Igor. First ruler to be baptized by Orthodox Church, then in Constantinople.

Svyatoslav (969-72) – A great warrior who conquered Bulgaria but neglected domestic affairs and was ultimately murdered.

Yaropolk (972-80) – Killed his brother in a power struggle and was later murdered by half-brother Vladimir.

Vladimir I (980-1015) – Established Russian Orthodox Church and strengthened Russia. Maintained a harem of five wives and countless concubines and was later canonized.

Yaroslav the Wise (1015-54) – Well-educated warrior and diplomat who fostered a cultural golden age in the capital of Kiev.

Various rulers (1054-1113) – Sons of Yaroslav and other would-be heirs fought amongst themselves, with power being passed around.

Vladimir II Monomakh (1113-25) – Benevolent ruler who took power at age sixty and united temporarily northern and southern principalities.

Various rulers (1125-55) – Squabbling amongst brothers and cousins divided the country once again and resulted in six short reigns.

Yury Dolgoruky (1155-57) – A power-hungry sort who founded Moscow and was later poisoned to death by his enemies.

Various rulers (1157-69) – Power struggles resulted in three or four short reigns and the burning of Kiev.

Andrey Bogolubov (1169-74) – Moved the capital from Kiev to Vladimir. Behaved unkindly to boyars, who later killed him and sacked his city.

Vsevolod III (1176-1212) – Known as the Big Nest due to his rather large family. Strengthened Vladimir-Suzdal principality, still the seat of the divided empire.

Various rulers (1212-52) – Descendants of Vsevolod were neutralized as invading Mongols massacred the Russian people and sacked their cities, establishing Golden Horde domination.

Alexander Nevsky (1252-63) – Famous warrior who defeated the Swedes on the Neva before being installed as grand prince. Was poisoned to death by Mongol-Tatars and later canonized.

Various rulers (1263-1328) – The Golden Horde manipulated family feuds. Relatives of Alexander Nevsky alternately took power and/or were killed.

Ivan I (1328-41) – Known as the Money Bags. Was installed as grand prince in new capital of Moscow. Placated the Golden Horde by being a good tax collector while embezzling on the sly.

Semyon (1341-53) – Intended to abate future power struggles by decreeing that only sons of princes were legitimate heirs. Unfortunately he had no sons when he died of plague.

Ivan II (1353-59) – Brother of Semyon. Managed to leave behind a son.

Dmitry Donskoy (1359-89) – Heroic ruler who handed the Golden Horde their first defeat, at Kulikovo. For some reason he wasn't canonized until 1989.

Vasily I (1389-1425) – Continued to resist Mongol-Tatars. Instituted last names for Russians, although his is unknown.

Vasily II (1425-62) – Known as the Dark because he was blinded by an opponent for paying an excessive sum to the Golden Horde to release him after being captured in battle.

Ivan III [the Great] (1462-1505) – Stood up to the crumbling Golden Horde, ending Russia's subjugation. Unified the Russian lands at last and built the Moscow Kremlin.

Vasily III (1505-33) – Mopped up remaining independent principalities for Muscovy. Has the dubious distinction of being Ivan the Terrible's father.

Ivan IV [the Terrible] (1533-84) – First ruler to take the title of tsar. Paranoid and murderous, he saved face by conquering Kazan, Astrakhan, and much of Siberia.

Fyodor I (1584-98) – Feeble-minded son of Ivan IV. He was a mere figurehead while brother-in-law Boris Godunov ruled the country. His death ended the Rurik dynasty.

Boris Godunov (1598-1605) – Allegedly orchestrated the murder of Fyodor's brother, Tsarevich Dmitry, thus gaining the throne and setting the stage for the Time of Troubles.

False Dmitry I (1605-06) – Claimed he was Tsarevich Dmitry alive after all. Mustered an army and stormed Moscow, taking the throne. Was eventually killed and, in a symbolic gesture, shot out of a cannon.

Vasily Shuisky (1606-10) – Boyar who organized an army and ousted False Dmitry I. Upset by the appearance of a second pretender, he had the real Dmitry exhumed and brought him to Moscow.

False Dmitry II (1608-10) – Also claiming to be Tsarevich Dmitry, he commenced to rule from a camp outside of Moscow but was soon killed by loyalists.

Throne vacant (1610-13) – The Time of Troubles reached its peak when the Poles occupied Moscow. They were eventually ousted by a Volga region army led by Minin and Pozharsky.

Michael Romanov (1613-45) – A young boyar distantly related to Ivan IV, he accepted the throne at the behest of a popular assembly. The first ruler of the Romanov dynasty.

Alexey (1645-76) – Known as the Quiet. Annexed the Ukraine and put down Stepan Razin's famous peasant revolt, apparently without making much noise.

Fyodor III (1676-82) – Achieved nothing earth-shattering. Has the distinction of being the half-brother of Peter the Great.

Ivan V (1682-96) – As a sickly boy he shared the throne with Peter I, although the country was ruled by the boys' sister, Regent Sofia, until Peter matured and elbowed her out.

Peter I [the Great] (1682-1725) – Turned Russia into a prominent European power and delivered her from cultural backwardness. Founded St. Petersburg, established the navy, won the Northern War, shaved beards, was fond of beheading, died of a bladder infection.

Catherine I (1725-27) – Peter's wife. She left the ruling up to Peter's right-hand man, Menshikov.

Peter II (1727-30) – Peter's grandson. Never ruled from the capital, staying in Moscow after his coronation. Died of smallpox shortly thereafter.

Anna (1730-40) – Peter the Great's niece. Surrounded herself with foreign advisors and executed opponents by the thousands. Decadent and repressive, she ran up the national debt by throwing lots of parties.

Ivan VI (1740-41) – Unfortunate two month-old tsar who was ousted in a coup and exiled. He was imprisoned later at Shlisselburg and killed during a failed rescue attempt.

Elizabeth (1741-61) – Peter the Great's daughter. Half-heartedly carried on her father's reforms. Was adored by the court for her excesses—she owned 15,000 dresses and liked to party all night.

Peter III (1761-62) – Relieved the nobility of compulsory 25-year state service, thus creating a privileged leisure class. Was ousted in a coup by his shrewd wife, future Catherine II.

Catherine II [the Great] (1762-96) – Increased Russia's cultural sophistication and power. Continued Westernization. Flirted with lifting repressions. Flirted with everything (though the horse rumor is doubtful).

Paul (1796-1801) – Catherine's son. Despised his mother and attempted to reverse her liberal policies. Was strangled in a palace coup sanctioned by his son, future Alexander I.

Alexander I (1801-25) – Was occupied mostly with foreign affairs, including Napoleon's invasion. He beat the French in 1812 by leaving them in Moscow right before winter.

Nicholas I (1825-55) – Put down Decembrists' revolt and thereafter ruled with an iron fist. A despot *par excellence*, he even declared himself Pushkin's personal censor.

Alexander II (1855-81) – Freed the serfs and pushed through a few other admirable reforms. Failed to satisfy emerging radical groups, though, and was killed by a bomb.

Alexander III (1881-94) – A reactionary ruler, likely influenced by his father's assassination. Passed anti-Semitic laws and watched Russia's industrialization foster worker malcontent.

Nicholas II (1894-1917) – The last tsar. Blundered on Bloody Sunday, the Russo-Japanese War, WWI, as well as internal affairs. Was shot along with his entire family soon after abdicating.

V. I. Lenin (1917-24) – Engineered the 1917 Revolution and founded the world's first socialist state. He championed true communism yet quickly resorted to dictatorship. Privately referred to Russians as "fools."

Josef Stalin (1929-53) – Brought the USSR to the forefront of industrialized nations, survived WWII, and committed mass genocide that made Hitler's seem unambitious. An extremely bad man.

Nikita Khrushchev (1957-64) – Denounced Stalin and embarked on limited human rights reforms. Blundered in foreign affairs, couldn't help the economy, and was "retired."

Leonid Brezhnev (1964-82) – Un-denounced Stalin and put an end to reforms. Thrived on bureaucracy and Stolichnaya as Soviet society steadily collected dust.

Yury Andropov (1982-84) – Conservative former KGB chief who began anti-corruption and anti-alcohol campaigns but died shortly thereafter.

Konstantin Chernenko (1984-85) – Described by *Newsweek* as Brezhnev's "chief pencil sharpener and bottle opener." Installed at age 73 to buy time for a scrambling Politburo.

Mikhail Gorbachev (1985-1991) – Embarked on unprecedented reforms. He started a train he couldn't stop, though, and the USSR and his job ceased to exist while he was on vacation.

Boris Yeltsin (1991-) – The first ever democratically elected ruler of Russia. Survived two coup attempts and now faces the Herculean task of lifting Russia out of the Third World. Doubtful he'll stay alive that long.

RUSSIAN HISTORY AT A GLANCE

Sure it's foolhardy to condense one thousand years of intrigue into a few pages. But who's got time for the unabridged version?

9th Century

Vikings, called Varangians, leave Scandinavia to establish trading settlements with Slavs existing in the Lake Ladoga and upper Volga regions. In 862 Norseman Rurik is "invited" to rule the Slavs' major northern settlement, which he calls Novgorod. The Russian state is born, as is the Rurik dynasty, which lasts until 1598. Rurik's relative and heir, Oleg, conquers Slavic-ruled Kiev two decades later, making the city the capital of a united empire called Rus.

10th Century

Vladimir I introduces feudalism and the Eastern Orthodox religion. The Church establishes its base in Kiev. Novgorod breaks off from Kiev. The divided empire consists of numerous principalities, independently ruled and quasi-democratic, although technically subservient to either Novgorod or Kiev.

11th Century

Kievan Rus enjoys a golden age under the rule of Yaroslav the Wise. The capital city is beautified on a Byzantine model. The first Russian Metropolitan is appointed, symbolizing the Russian Orthodox Church's growing independence from Constantinople. In the north Novgorod remains a powerful independent center of mercantilism and religion.

12th Century

Benevolent ruler Vladimir II Monomakh unites the empire for a brief period in the early century. He founds the city of Vladimir in the Rostov-Suzdal region, placing it under the rule of his son, Yury Dolgoruky (the Long-armed). Under Yury Dolgoruky, the Rostov-Suzdal principality grows powerful, although the northern principalities, including Novgorod, once again splinter off. In an effort to expand and protect his domain, Yury founds the city of Moscow in 1147. Rostov-Suzdal continues to flourish to the extent that Yury's son, Andrey Bogolubov, sacks Kiev and moves the capital of Rus to Vladimir. The Church remains in Kiev.

13th Century

Mongols led by Genghis Khan thunder out of Asia and invade the Caucasus as well as the Volga and Don plains located south of the Russian principalities. They continue north and trounce the Russian princedoms until Genghis Khan suddenly dies. His grandson Batu Khan finishes the job with a vengeance, laying waste to every town from Kiev to Moscow. The Golden Horde, a khanate of the Mongol-Tatar empire, rules the

Russian principalities until the 15th century from their base of Saray (near present day Volgograd) on the lower Volga. The Horde controls all local governments, appointing Russian princes to collect taxes. The Russians suffer a subjugation they never forget.

Prince Alexander of Novgorod defeats invading Swedes at the Neva River, earning the title Alexander Nevsky (of the Neva). The Golden Horde installs Alexander as the grand prince of Rus, seated in Vladimir. His son Daniil is declared prince of Muscovy, the principality centered around Moscow. The Church moves to Vladimir.

14th Century

The seat of the empire is moved to the Muscovy principality. Ivan I (the Moneybags), known for his energetic tax-collecting, is installed as grand prince. The Church also moves to Moscow. The Muscovy principality grows wealthy, as Ivan the Moneybags is also adept at embezzling. Later in the century Grand Prince Dmitry attacks the weakening Golden Horde, winning a historic battle at Kulikovo on the Don River. The heroic grand prince earns the name Dmitry Donskoy (of the Don). Muscovy continues to grow powerful, annexing the Rostov-Suzdal principality. The Golden Horde strikes back, however, violently ransacking the country true to form, enslaving nearly one million Russians, and retaining control of Rus. The nationalist effort is put on hold.

15th Century

Under Vasily I and Vasily II, Muscovy continues to resist Mongol-Tatar domination, although squabbling among principalities still divides the country. Ivan III (the Great) finally refuses to pay tribute to the Golden Horde, thus ending over two centuries of subjugation. Massive expansion follows. Ivan annexes major principalities, including Novgorod, to Muscovy and claims large portions of the Ural Mountains. The country at last stands more or less unified and five times greater in size than before Ivan's reign. With Constantinople falling to the Turks, the Russian Church becomes fully independent, and Moscow is declared the "third Rome," the true heir of Christianity. The city and Kremlin are rebuilt in a grand Byzantine style, and Muscovy adopts the former Byzantine crest of a double-headed eagle, which remains the symbol of the monarchy until 1917.

16th Century

Ivan III's grandson Ivan IV (the Terrible) is the first ruler to crown himself tsar of all Russia, which is now referred to as Muscovy or Great Rus. Ivan conquers the once mighty Tatar strongholds of Kazan and Astrakhan, thereby gaining for Great Rus the entire Volga region as well as access to the Caspian Sea and Siberia. However, after the 25 year-long Livonian War with Poland and Sweden, Ivan remains unable to claim the

Baltic lands. Known to be rather violent and paranoid, Ivan sacks Novgorod, snuffing out that city's golden age. In a fit of rage he kills his oldest son, Ivan, heir to the throne. Upon Ivan IV's death the throne is inherited by his second son, Fyodor I. Rather slow mentally, Fyodor is controlled by brother-in-law Boris Godunov, acting as regent. Boris Godunov allegedly orchestrates the murder of Fyodor's half-brother Tsarevich Dmitry in Uglich, thus setting the stage for his own uncontested ascension to the throne. Fyodor's death in 1598 marks the end of the Rurik dynasty, and Boris Godunov takes the throne.

17th Century

Widespread famine and peasant uprisings usher in the century and the Time of Troubles. In 1604, with the death of Boris Godunov one year away, a Russian monk named Grigory living in Poland claims to be Tsarevich Dmitry, not murdered in Uglich after all. Discontented boyars as well as the Polish army back the pretender, who marches on Moscow. He kills Boris Godunov's son, on the throne following Boris's death, and proclaims himself tsar. Known as False Dmitry I, he rules for a year before being overthrown and killed by a loyalist army led by boyar Vasily Shuisky, who takes the throne. Another pretender appears, also claiming to be Dmitry and also claiming power. The Poles take advantage of the instability and occupy Moscow. Eventually a popular army led by Minin and Pozharsky evicts the Poles. in 1613 a young boyar named Michael Romanov is chosen by an Assembly of the Land to take the throne. The Time of Troubles ends; the 200 year-long Romanov dynasty begins.

Michael's successor, Alexey, makes large territorial gains, including the Ukraine and Siberia. He also turns serfs into slaves by proclaiming them unattached to their estates. Cossack Stepan Razin leads the country's largest ever peasant revolt, which is ultimately subdued. In 1689 Peter I (the Great) seizes power from his sister-regent, although he doesn't begin ruling with interest for another five years. Russia stands on the threshold of a new century and a remarkable reign.

18th Century

Peter the Great founds St. Petersburg in 1703, moving the capital there from Moscow nine years later. The city, designed on a European model, is destined to flourish as the political and cultural center of Russia for the next 200 years. Peter force-feeds Western culture to Russia, fostering unprecedented advances as well as resentment. The country's first navy is instrumental in finally subduing the Swedes in the Northern War and gaining the Baltic territories.

After a series of relatively ineffectual rulers (Catherine I, Peter II, Anna, Ivan VI, Elizabeth, Peter III), the torch is passed to Catherine the Great, who continues to cultivate Western influences throughout Russia. The arts and sciences thrive like never before, although a newly formed class of critical elite begins to vocally oppose the monarchy. A Cossack named Pugachev leads the country's most violent peasant uprising but ends up captured and hanged. Various military campaigns result in the annexation of the Crimea, Lithuania, and Byelorussia. Catherine's son, Paul, inherits the throne before the close of the century. He attempts to undo everything associated with Catherine but is murdered in an 1801 coup.

19th Century

Under Alexander I, Russia annexes Georgia, Azerbaijan, Bessarabia, and Finland. In 1812 Napoleon invades Russia, occupying Moscow. The city burns, but Alexander refuses to negotiate with Napoleon, forcing the French to retreat. They are chased back to Paris and ultimately surrender. Alexander's death in 1825 sparks a protest for reform staged by officers and aristocrats. Known as Decembrists, the protesters are subdued and either hanged or exiled by Alexander's successor, Nicholas I. Under his military-minded, repressive rule, the country nonetheless enjoys economic growth. Pushkin, Lermontov, and Gogol define Russian national literature, which is soon to be expanded by Dostoyevsky and Turgenev.

Alexander II, son of Nicholas I, abolishes serfdom in 1861, although on terms that fail to appease the masses. A market economy and industrial expansion ensue, with urban working classes springing up in suburbs of major cities. Karl Marx's *Das Kapital* is translated into Russian, spawning Marxist groups which take their place among other radical, reform-minded factions. Russia sells Alaska to America for 7.2 million dollars. Alexander is assassinated in 1881, although the event fails to stir up the expected uprising. Alexander's son, Alexander III, rules for the next 13 years, repressing revolutionaries and escaping a major assassination attempt. Nicholas II, the last Russian tsar, takes the throne in 1894.

20th Century

Peaceful protesters are massacred by tsarist troops in a 1905 debacle called Bloody Sunday, egging on political discontent and social unrest. Nicholas II offers half-hearted concessions to activists calling for democratic representation. Workers councils called *soviets* are set up in St. Petersburg and Moscow. World War I drains the economy and absorbs the tsar, who steadily loses control over the people and abdicates in 1917. A provisional government is formed.

The Bolsheviks, calling for all power to the Soviets, overthrow the provisional government in the 1917 October Revolution. Led by Lenin, they confiscate all private, royal, and Church holdings and create a Constituent Assembly, to be elected democratically. However, the Bolsheviks win a minority of seats in the first election. Using force, they dissolve the Assembly, nipping representational government in the bud.

Lenin moves the capital of Russia back to Moscow, changing the name of the Bolshevik Party to the Communist Party. Foreign Affairs Minister Trotsky signs the Treaty of Brest, getting Russia out of WWI by ceding Finland, Poland, the Baltics, the Ukraine, and the Caucasus. Censorship, bans on strikes, and seizure of agriculture are implemented to consolidate the "War Communism" effort against mounting internal opposition. Various factions, referred to as White Guards, oppose the Communists (Red Guards), and bloody civil war rages throughout the country for the next three years. Famine kills five million people. Russia is renamed the Union of Soviet Socialist Republics in 1922. Lenin dies two years later, after having purged Party membership, setting a precedent for his successor, Josef Stalin.

Stalin outmaneuvers rivals and asserts supremacy as general secretary. He shrewdly orchestrates a personality cult around Lenin. Forced collectivization of all farms is implemented; peasants unwilling to surrender their farms are shipped off to labor camps by the millions. Proliferation of heavy industry becomes the country's main goal, and Russia is transformed from a floundering agricultural nation to a global industrial leader. In the thirties Stalin purges massive numbers of party members, military leaders, and intellectuals. Millions are executed or sent to labor camps now called GULAG. WWII, called the "Great Patriotic War," costs the country 25 million lives. Victory results in the Soviet Union's regaining the Ukraine and Baltic States and setting up communist puppet governments throughout Eastern Europe. The Cold War begins. Purges continue after the war. The final death toll of Stalin's reign of terror is figured to be as high as 30 million. The most murderous dictator the world has ever known dies in 1953.

Nikita Khrushchev takes power and denounces Stalin in his "secret speech" to the Twentieth Party Congress. Repressions are mildly alleviated and the country enjoys a brief intellectual and cultural "thaw." Cosmonaut Yury Gagarin becomes the first man in space. The Cuban missile crisis, rift with China, economic failure, and other setbacks cost Khrushchev his job in 1964. Under Khrushchev's successor, Leonid Brezhnev, the Soviet Union invades Czechoslovakia in 1968 and Afghanistan in 1979. In between, repression continues, and economic stagnation plagues the country. While urbanites reside in communal flats and stand in bread lines, the Party elite enjoy special privileges and comparatively lavish lifestyles. Cynical malaise pervades the populace. Brezhnev dies in 1982. Former KGB chief Yury Andropov succeeds Brezhnev but dies three years later. Konstantin Chernenko steps in for less than a year before kicking the bucket in 1985.

Fifty-four year-old Mikhail Gorbachev emerges as general secretary. Championing a new style of leadership, he aims to revive the economy and make peace with the West. He introduces *glasnost* (openness) and *perestroika* (restructuring). Political prisoners and exiles, including Nobel laureate Andrey Sakharov, are freed. Quasi-democratic elections are held for seats in the Congress of People's Deputies (Parliament), but Party members hold onto the majority. Boris Yeltsin becomes parliamentary chairman. He tears up his Communist Party card and proclaims independence of the Russian state, mimicking gestures already made by several republics. A failed coup attempt by Party hard-liners in August 1991 results in the dissolution of the Communist Party and the collapse of the Soviet Union.

Boris Yeltsin gains effective control of the Russian government. Gorbachev officially steps down four months later. Yeltsin's goal is to introduce full-blown democracy and capitalism. Privatization of state enterprises commences. Ill-prepared for a free market system, the post-Soviet economy worsens. Gridlock between the parliamentary and executive branches paralyzes Yeltsin's reforms and ratification of his new constitution. In September 1993 Yeltsin dissolves Parliament, calling for free elections. Former Yeltsin allies lead a group of deputies who refuse to vacate the White House. They advocate armed rebellion, and street fighting breaks out in Moscow. The army, after some wavering, remains loyal to Yeltsin and bombards the White House with tankfire, ending another coup attempt. In December 1993 the first truly multi-party elections are held for Parliament. Hoping to gain a cooperative parliamentary contingency, Yeltsin suffers a crushing setback when Neo-Fascists, led by radical nationalist Vladimir Zhirinovsky, and Communists gain a majority of seats. The Russian Constitution, including a Bill of Rights is ratified, however. Yeltsin maintains effective control of the government, and economic reforms push onward as debilitating inflation and the ever-plummeting ruble continue to dash the public's hopes for a new and improved Russia.

SOUVENIR BUYING GUIDE

Here are some pointers to help you get the most for your money while acquiring keepsakes of your trip to Russia.

SOUVENIRS AND COLLECTIBLES

First of all, forget anything you might have heard at home about using American cigarettes as currency or engaging in profitable bartering with your own t-shirts or blue-jeans. Those days have past. Marlboros and Levi's have long been available in Russian shops and kiosks, and foreign t-shirts hold only marginal interest for serious souvenir vendors. It's a hardened market now, and like most other places in the world, money talks loudest.

Second of all, as of January 1994 all businesses in Russia are prohibited from selling goods for foreign "hard" currencies (with the exception of establishments conducting credit card transactions). Hard currency still is greatly coveted, but offering US dollars to street vendors does not necessarily gain you any bargaining leverage. Prices in rubles are carefully tied to the dollar, and peddlers implement their own exchange rates. You therefore end up spending about the same amount no matter what your form of payment. If you have brought a bevy of goods from home with which to barter, it can't hurt to use them in your negotiations, but don't expect them to be valued like gold.

In terms of where to find the greatest selections, highest levels of quality, and cheapest prices, exceptions prove the rule. You simply never know. In Moscow and St. Petersburg prices on the streets and at flea markets tend to be better than those in tourist shops. Selection on the streets can also be as great as that in the shops. However, shops can provide good deals on items not available on the streets. And vice versa. Western hotels naturally ask the most exorbitant prices for souvenirs and other goods, but offer the advantage of accepting credit cards. The souvenir kiosk on your ship can actually be one of your best bets, as it can offer competitive prices, a thoughtful selection, and unbeatable convenience. In the provinces one would expect to find the best deals, but oftentimes the prices are higher than in the cities. Variety is definitely more limited in small towns, but you might find a unique chess set in Uglich, for example, that you will not see anywhere else. Items associated with specific places, like a book on Kizhi Island for example, are of course best purchased at the source. To repeat, exceptions prove the rule; you simply never know.

The best rule of thumb is this: If something strikes your fancy, buy it. You might pass up a lot of appealing things along the way in hopes of doing better at your final destination of either Moscow or St. Petersburg, only to end up being short of time and unable to find what you want once there. If you buy a painted tray in Petrozavodsk only to find the identical tray in Moscow for a few thousand rubles less, so what? And if you find a much nicer lacquer box in St. Petersburg than the one you already bought back in Yaroslavl, you can always give the bad one to Aunt Myrtle—and she will love it.

Painted lacquer boxes are a staple on the souvenir shopping list. Because they range from cheap trinkets to valuable pieces of art, it is important to know how to distinguish an authentic one from a fake. Be aware that whether in an expensive shop or on a back-alley souvenir table, well-crafted boxes can sit right next to bad imitations—and to the untrained eye the imitation can even seem more appealing. For everything you need to know about lacquer boxes, we recommend visiting the web site <www.sunbirds.com>. The outfit is run by folks who actually used to run one of the best ship gift kiosks, and their on-line catalogue of boxes is unparalleled.

Genuine hand-painted boxes come from only four villages in Russia: Palekh, Fedoskino, Mstera, and Kholui. The name of the village as well as that of the artist (both in

Cyrillic) should be painted on the box itself. Each village is known for its distinct manner of painting. Artists from Palekh are renowned for using gold leaf in rendering highly detailed and intricate scenes. The background is a rich black, so when you're looking at a lot of gold ornamentation on a deep black background, you're looking at Palekh. Fedoskino painters incorporate mother of pearl either in their pigments or directly on their boxes, thus their work is identified by a unique iridescence. The trademark Fedoskino scene is a "tea party" depicting two bearded men at a table with a samovar. Mstera artisans make liberal use of blue tones, which in general make their painting distinctly colorful. Painters from Kholui tend to render their scenes in a comparatively flat manner.

There are two main types of impostor boxes. The first are those that actually are not painted at all, but instead bear a print touched up with paint. The second are those that are simply poorly executed by untrained artists not hailing from one of the above-mentioned villages. Using a magnifying glass (often furnished by respectable dealers) is the best way to judge a box's quality. Questions to ask yourself: Does the scene look like it was clipped from a magazine and pasted onto the box (i.e., is there no visible black background and no evidence of brushwork)? Is the brushwork meticulous or sloppy (i.e., is careful attention paid to shading or is the paint merely blobbed on)? Are the designs or scenes on the sides of the box rendered in the same style as that of the picture on top? Do the pieces of the box fit together properly? Is it really a paper mâché box, or is it plastic?

Many excellent boxes are collectors items and fetch thousands of dollars. Others that are indeed well done and genuine can be had for thirty to sixty dollars. Minuscule boxes can be more expensive than larger ones simply because of the skill involved in painting on them. Boxes with painting on all sides are naturally more expensive than those painted only on top. If you're looking at a box as an investment, then be absolutely certain of its authenticity. If you want a box as a simple memento, then you are much freer, for even crude fakes can exhibit a desirable charm.

The ubiquitous Russian nesting dolls called *matryoshkas* are also a mandatory purchase. Although the guidelines for identifying quality ones are not as involved as those for lacquer boxes, most of the same rules apply. Simply inspect the craftsmanship. The more skillfully painted the dolls, the more valuable they are. And naturally the more dolls to a set, the more costly it is. Beware of cheap *matryoshkas* that are churned out in factories or in mass-production workshops. If after close inspection of all the pieces, you find yourself enchanted with the workmanship, then go ahead and pop the question, "*Skolko stoit* (how much)?"

Even if you're no Gary Kasparov, a Russian **chess set** makes a wonderful acquisition, for displayed at home it exudes an exotic as well as intellectual aura. Hand-painted chess sets are the norm. Although few sets are genuine pieces of art, the majority are delightfully colorful and playfully painted. The big thing to look out for is the material used, which ought to be wood. Even if the board and all the pieces seem to be made of wood, double check the knights, which are often painted-over plastic molds. In a nice chess set, all of the men should be carved, including the more complicated knights. In the cities you can occasionally find exquisite chess sets made in various Asian republics such as Kirghizia. These sets are meticulously painted and carved, and utilize a variety of exotic wood. They're comparatively expensive, but usually worth far more than what you pay.

Russian **watches** are an increasingly popular tourist item. There is certainly no Rolex equivalent in Russia, but a variety of unique and fairly reliable timepieces are available. Mechanically speaking, three types of watches are available: quartz, automatic, and wind-up. Quartz watches can't be wound; mechanical watches are wound by wrist movement; and wind-up watches are, well, wound by twisting the knob. Although a novelty to the Swatch generation, the latter variety represents your best bet. It can be a problem replacing the battery of a Russian quartz watch at home, and mechanical watches are the most prone to break. A good old-fashioned wind-up, however, can last you a lifetime.

The most valuable and reliable of the wind-ups are the authentic Russian military watches. These are large watches with a good weight and 17-jewel movement. They are also waterproof to a depth of fifty meters. Their faces come in a variety of colors and styles, depending on their armed forces association; they also bear a small emblem of either a tank, a submarine, a parachute, a ship, a jet, or a red star. When buying a military watch, make sure it runs well, make sure the back is authentic (well-sealed and engraved with a pattern of lines), and make sure you get a leather band thrown in.

Be advised that any genuine antiques, especially **icons** and wood-burning **samovars**, are bound to bring you big trouble at customs.

CONSUMABLE FARE

Knowing how to buy **caviar** seems to evade most tourists. Aficionados who know the difference between the three main varieties (*osetr*, *sevruga*, and *beluga*) will have to hunt through specialty markets and state fish shops in the major cities to find that coveted tin full of the large grayish eggs specific to a genuine *beluga* sturgeon. Everybody else must decide what to do with all those tins and jars offered by the kids at the side of the ship. Here is the answer: Do not buy any caviar that has not been kept perpetually refrigerated since its original packaging. Real caviar, which comes only from sturgeons, spoils if it is not kept constantly cool. Therefore if you want to sample caviar in good condition, forget about buying virtually all the caviar you see on the streets. (If you don't care about the condition of the eggs, however, go ahead and buy caviar off the street—it is entirely edible, just hopelessly dried-out. In fact, if you have friends at home who won't know the difference between dried-out and well-kept caviar, you may as well buy a few gifts.)

Red "caviar" technically is not caviar at all, as it comes from salmon. It is, however, cheaper than black and quite tasty in its own right. Plus it is not nearly as fragile, so you can get away with buying it just about anywhere you find it.

If you want to experience the real thing, though, you'll have to buy your caviar from a bar, restaurant, or shop. And you'll have to eat it while in Russia, as you won't be able to get it home without spoiling it. If the container bears the word "*malossol*" it contains pretty good roe, as *malossol* means "a little salt," a characteristic of good caviar. Also, if you want to look like a connoisseur, forget the bread, the crackers, the chopped onions, and the sour cream, and eat your caviar with nothing but a spoon.

Russian **vodka** is more durable than caviar, although there are many impostor brands, some of which are pure lighter fluid. Following a few simple buying guidelines, though, will allow you to taste for yourself the acclaimed spirit that gets the Russians through their Arctic winters.

By now many foreign vodkas have invaded the market to cater to the vast majority of Russians who believe that anything produced outside their country, including their famed national spirit, is superior to the native-made product. Imported brands often have Russian-sounding names, so we recommend sticking to these established Russian brands: *Stolichnaya, Russkaya, Moskovskaya, Pyatizvezdochnaya* (our favorite), *Pertsovka* (pepper-flavored), *Limonnaya* (lemon-flavored), and *Pshenichnaya* (tasty wheat vodka). Two exceptional brands found only in

St. Petersburg are *Pyotr Velikiy* (Peter the Great) and *Sankt-Peterburg* (St. Petersburg).

More important, Russian authorities officially advise buying vodka only from stores, not from kiosks. Poisonous or just plain bad vodka is increasingly appearing on the streets. The ultimate test for distinguishing real vodka from plain spirit (or something more dangerous) is to shake the bottle and scrutinize the bubbles. Real vodka produces snaking, pinpoint bubbles which remain visible for a while. If what you see resembles more of a snowstorm full of big bubbles, you might want to save that bottle for the boss.

To be like a real Russian, only drink your vodka from a *ryumka* (shot glass) and in one gulp. Proposing a toast, perhaps more than anywhere else in the world, is essential before downing your shot—each time, no matter how many rounds you have. The standard toast is *za zdoroviye* ("to your health"). But one may insert anything he wants after the *za* ("to") in order to change the honoree. Thus other variants might be *za kapitana* ("to the captain") and, for those trying to make time with the pretty interpreters on board, *za dam* ("to the ladies").

Other popular beverages include beer and "cognac." Formerly, Russian beer was always locally brewed, without pasteurization, and thus required drinking within a few days of production. These days Russian breweries are catching up with the West. The most popular brand in all of Russia, the St. Petersburg-based Baltika, now produces seven grades of their tasty pasteurized beer and distribute it all across the country. Russian "cognacs," although in no way related to the real thing, can be enjoyable and are quite cheap. Georgian "cognac" is better than Russian, and Armenian "cognac" is considered the *crème de la crème* of Eastern European brandies. Russian wines are hopeless, although some Georgian and Moldavian wines can be palatable.

KEY TO PHOTOGRAPHS

(1) Personal shrine of the tsars. Annunciation Cathedral, Moscow.

(2) The obligatory image. St. Basil's Cathedral, Moscow.

(3) Children gather at the edge of a lock to collect gum and candy from ship passengers. Moscow Canal.

(4) Girls of Uglich.

(5) Boys of Kostroma.

(6) A sleepy town and ancient kremlin create an idyllic setting. Transfiguration Cathedral, Uglich.

(7) A ship passenger receives a gift in Kostroma.

(8) Star-studded cupolas from the 17th century. Church of St. Dmitry on the Blood, Uglich.

(9) Above the Golden Ring. From the top of the belfry inside the Savior-Transfiguration Monastery, Yaroslavl.

(10) No churches, just real people to meet during a "green stop" at the village of Irma.

(11) Hanging out beside walls of history. Outside the Monastery of St. Cyril of the White Lake, Kirillov.

(12) Endearing wrinkles of time. Lifelong resident of the Resurrection Convent, Goritsy.

(13) Look, mom, no nails! Transfiguration Cathedral, Kizhi Island.

(14) Pastoral setting, intriguing sights. Kizhi Island.

(15) Icons, icons, and more icons ...

(16) Natural preserve of Valaam Island.

(17) Ancient Orthodox outpost. Transfiguration Monastery, Valaam Island.

(18) "Venice of the North." Griboyedov Canal and Savior on the Blood Cathedral, St. Petersburg.

(19) Regal splendor. Catherine's Palace, city of Pushkin.